MORE ALIVE
WITH COLOR

LEATRICE EISEMAN

ALSO BY LEATRICE EISEMAN

THE PANTONE BOOK OF COLOR

COLORS FOR YOUR EVERY MOOD

PANTONE GUIDE TO COMMUNICATING WITH COLOR

THE COLOR ANSWER BOOK

A CAPITAL LIFESTYLES BOOK—OTHER BOOKS IN THE SERIES INCLUDE:

The Best Friends' Guide to Getting Fit by Kim Murphy and Kris Carpenter

Colorfully Slim: The 7-Day Color Diet and Lifetime Health Plan by Mindy Weisel et al.

Gathering in the Garden: Recipes and Ideas for Garden Parties by Shelley Snow and Elaine Husband

Mistakes Men Make that Women Hate: 101 Style Tips for Men by Ken Karpinski

Tea & Etiquette: Taking Tea for Business and Pleasure by Dorothea Johnson

MORE ALIVE
WITH COLOR

PERSONAL COLORS—PERSONAL STYLE
LEATRICE EISEMAN

A CAPITAL LIFESTYLES BOOK

CAPITAL
BOOKS, INC.
Sterling, Virginia

INQUIRIES SHOULD BE ADDRESSED TO:

Capital Books, Inc.

P.O. Box 605

Herndon, Virginia 20172-0605

ISBN 1-933102-09-8 (alk.paper)

ISBN 978-1-933102-09-2

Library of Congress Cataloging-in-Publication Data

Eiseman, Leatrice.

More alive with color : personal colors, personal style /

Leatrice Eiseman.– 1st ed.

    p. cm.

"A Capital lifestyles book."

Includes bibliographical references and index.

ISBN 1-933102-09-8 (hardcover)

1. Color in clothing. 2. Beauty, Personal.

3. Fashion. 4. Clothing and dress. I. Title.

    TT507.E34 2006

    646'.34--dc22

                                            2005019841

Printed on acid-free paper that meets the American National
Standards Institute Z39-48 Standard.

First Edition

10 9 8 7 6 5 4 3 2 1

Printed in China

THE PANTONE® SHOPPING COLOR GUIDE
A Portable Color Guide for Matching Color Choices

Pantone, Inc. empowers today's consumer to utilize the language
of color in much the same way that professional designers have
for the last four decades. With the PANTONE shopping color
guide, consumers can now carry with them a portable color
guide giving them a more precise way of communicating their
color choices and selecting the products in their lives.

Consumers of home and fashion products have a long
acquaintance with paint chips, magazine clippings, catalogs,
and rug and fabric swatches for coordinating the colors of their
prospective purchases. Now, with the PANTONE shopping color
guide, customers can bring a portable color memory to their point
of purchase. The PANTONE shopping color guide is available
through Pantone's website (www.pantoneuniverse.com).

THANK HUE!

My many thanks to all of those people who were so helpful in making this book a reality. First, to my longtime publisher and friend, Kathleen Hughes, for her patience, guidance, and vision on all things colorful. To Lisa Herbert, Pantone's Executive Vice President of Textile, Home, and Fashion for her cooperation, thoughtfulness, and great taste in all things design-related. To Bobbie Hawkes, my patient and multi-talented "right hand." To Cathy Neidermeyer and Diane Spera for their great "eyes." And to Sean Zindren for his wonderful art direction.

And to my colorful husband, Herb, for his encouragement and enthusiasm in supporting this book as well as my many other colorful passions.

CONTENTS

a personal note

Capital Books and I are very proud to bring a new generation *More Alive with Color* by the world's most illustrious color expert, Leatrice Eiseman. Lee and I have worked together on several color books. In fact, we launched our respective careers in color with her very first book, *Alive with Color*, on which this book is based. I was her editor at Acropolis Books, her first publisher—back when everyone was just beginning to get our "colors done." Acropolis had also published *Color Me Beautiful*, the international bestseller that popularized color and fashion theory. But even then, I recognized that Lee's Colortime system was more "inclusive"—offering broader palettes of color to a greater diversity of people.

Lee was ahead of her time when *Alive With Color* helped to start the color analysis movement. Since then she has gone on to help millions of people all over the world choose the best colors for their personal image and influenced the colors that everything from computers to toasters come in. For her work as a color guru, she has been named as one of the top fifty international style makers, as well as one of the most influential decision makers in business by *Fortune* magazine.

Now that the world is so much more aware of the many beautiful colors that people represent, *More Alive with Color* with its marvelous spectrum of colors geared to all types of skin, hair, and eye colors is even more "color timely." Everyone can understand how colors change with the shifting light of morning, noon, and night—making Lee's Colortime system of organizing personal colors the most versatile way to build a wardrobe and a style in tune with today's consumers.

Recently, Lee met a woman from Indonesia in one of her color workshops. This woman told her that she had always had a problem with the old seasonal color theory because it put all Indonesians into the Winter category and did not really recognize all the differences of coloring within

from the publisher

that culture. She said that she used the Sunrise, Sunlight, and Sunset palettes of Lee's Colortime system, as it gave her more colors to use in her personal wardrobe, but that also in her part of the world, people don't understand the differences in the seasons. They can't relate to winter, autumn, spring since it is always summer there! But everyone relates to the differences of color at various times of day.

So now we have *More Alive with Color* to give us more freedom in the colors we choose, something that contemporary consumers all over the world demand. We no longer want to be put into color boxes, we want to be able to expand our horizons. Lee's Colortime system offers us a greater understanding of the colors that we look best in, but also those that give our personality a chance to shine forth—no matter where we live or the skin and culture into which we were born. All are appreciated and celebrated in *More Alive with Color.*

We invite you into the new world of color, and the new way of thinking about how to use it in your life. In these pages, you'll learn more about how color can influence your emotions and how you feel—not only as you organize your closet for looking your best, dress for a job interview with confidence, or pack your suitcase for an important business trip or a restful vacation; but also why you've always felt happiest in lilac, or yellow, or lime green, or whatever color you fancy. Now you'll understand why you might not have been happy when you "had your colors done" years ago. You'll have a chance to expand your personal colors into a personal style that is YOU.

Thank you, Lee, from all of us who love color.

Kathleen Hughes, publisher, CAPITAL BOOKS

why I wrote this book

I am a confessed color addict! Colors affect my mood and sense of well-being. In looking back, I realize that my mother's passion for the paintbrush must have been a major influence in my life. Almost every year, she would go through the house painting everything in sight that didn't move, including the piano. I don't know how the people who bought that piano years later moved it out of the house. It must have weighed a ton with those twenty-five-odd (some of them very odd) coats of paint!

One year she outdid herself by painting an old metal toaster a not terribly attractive chartreuse. Someone mistakenly used it and the house reeked of smoke for weeks. My mother retired from painting for a while after that, so we lived with chartreuse for a long time. But ultimately her need to reinvent the colors won out.

In college, art and psychology were two of my favorite subjects. I devoured information on color. I read, studied, and researched every color-related topic I could get my hands on. In my early career as director of education for a group of self-improvement schools, when I researched curriculum and trained the teachers, color was invariably the subject that claimed most of my attention.

Presently, as an author, director of the Pantone Color Institute®, color forecaster, and consultant, I deliver seminars internationally for universities, professional organizations, trade shows, and conventions, and I consult with a variety of industries. My audiences and clients are diverse. They include interior designers and contractors; industrial, fashion, and graphic designers; for packaging, manufacturers, printers, retailers, florists, marketing and image consultants, as well as consumers—people interested in color, which includes just about everyone! Although they come from diverse areas, they have one thing in common: they are fascinated with color and understand its importance and impact.

One of the most important things I have learned about color is that you never stop learning about it, because color "rules" are never so rigid that they cannot be adapted to your needs. If you already have a real sense of color, you'll find that this book helps you understand why you choose the colors you do. If you are a professional who deals with color, it may open new avenues of thinking—such as how to deal more objectively with your clients. If you are really interested in color, you'll not only find out about the "how-to's," but also about the "why-do-I's" of the colors you choose.

The purpose of this book is to share my discoveries with you so that you can enrich your life, as I have mine, and learn to be more alive with color! Color can literally change your life and can certainly simplify it.

Among the things you will learn here are how to:

1. Use color to make you feel more secure and successful.
2. Take advantage of your personal Signature Colors.
3. Avoid expensive mistakes with color.
4. Use color—with confidence—to bring out your creativity.
5. Understand what goes with what and why.
5. Discover what color says about you.
6. Use my Color Clock system to simplify, organize, and excite your life!

Learn all of this and more in the pages that follow.

part 1

what color can do for you

1

THE COLOR QUIZ

Have you ever wished that choosing colors were easier? Or wondered why you love the way you look in some colors but not in others? This quiz will help you understand why you like certain colors and why those colors look best on you. It will introduce you to my Color Clock system which is divided into three Colortime palettes that reflect the natural colors of morning (Sunrise), midday (Sunlight), and early evening (Sunset). Based on your eye, hair, and skin color (not the time of day you like best), take this quiz and discover which of these Colortime palettes contains the personal colors that define your style.

QUESTION 1

Look at the photographs on the bottom of this page. Which photograph contains the colors that appeal to you most?

Answer the following questions without stopping to analyze your responses. Don't stop to think; let your answers reflect your immediate reaction to color.

CHECK ONE: ☐ SUNRISE   ☒ SUNSET   ☐ SUNLIGHT

Now look at the three Colortime palettes in chapter 2. Which palette represents the group of colors you like most? Don't choose them on the basis of one particular color or the colors that you think are most popular now. Choose the Colortime palette you really like best. Get a sense of the whole picture and how the colors look together.

CHECK ONE: ☒ SUNRISE   ☐ SUNSET   ☐ SUNLIGHT

QUESTION 2

If you could buy an entirely new wardrobe, which Colortime palette has most of the colors you would choose to wear?

CHECK ONE: ☐ SUNRISE   ☐ SUNSET   ☒ SUNLIGHT

QUESTION 3

If you could completely redecorate your home, which Colortime palette has most of the colors you would choose?

CHECK ONE: ☐ SUNRISE   ☒ SUNSET   ☐ SUNLIGHT

SUNRISE   SUNSET   SUNLIGHT

PHOTOS: DON PAULSON

QUESTION 4

If you are unsure about these answers, don't worry. Just pick the answer you think comes closest to describing your coloring.

Look at yourself in a mirror, near natural light if possible. Then answer the following questions to determine your personal coloring. Make the best selections you can from the choices given or ask a friend to help you. Mark your answers and tally the results.

What Is Your Eye Color?

Blue

Sunrise Blue

❑ SUNRISE	Pure blue, cool clear light blue, medium blue, or blue-gray
❑ SUNSET	Mid or deep blue (often with warm flecks of color)
❑ SUNLIGHT	Blue, but change depending on the color I'm wearing

Brown

Sunset Brown

❑ SUNRISE	Rosy brown (light, medium, or dark), very dark brown, almost jet black
☒ SUNSET	Amber, warm golden brown (light, medium, or dark)
❑ SUNLIGHT	Brown, but I don't see myself in any one of the above categories as I seem to be a combination of several colors

Hazel

Sunlight Green

❑ SUNRISE	Gray hazel (a combination of blue, gray, and some green)
❑ SUNSET	Golden hazel (a combination of brown, gold, green, and perhaps some blue)
❑ SUNLIGHT	Hazel, but I don't see myself distinctly in any of the above categories because I have many colors in my eyes

Green

Each Colortime has eye colors of blue, brown, hazel, and green; but they vary in warmth, clarity, and depth of color.

❑ SUNRISE	Bright blue-green
❑ SUNSET	Green with golden flecks
❑ SUNLIGHT	Light or medium blue-green, but I don't see myself distinctly in any of the above categories

What Is Your Hair Color?

If you color your hair, answer this question based on your natural hair color.

Blonde

❏ SUNRISE	Ash or sandy blonde (light, medium or dark), platinum blonde or towhead
❏ SUNSET	Golden, honey, or coppery blonde (light, medium or dark)
❏ SUNLIGHT	Blonde (light, medium, or dark), but I don't see myself as being any of the above. I think I have a mixture of the blondes, both warm and cool tones together

Red

❏ SUNRISE	Auburn, with cool blue undertones
❏ SUNSET	Golden copper red (light, medium or dark), rust-wine red, like Bordeaux
❏ SUNLIGHT	Red, but I I have a combination of both warm and cool tones

Brown

❏ SUNRISE	Ash brown (light, medium or dark, but without gold), dark brown, may have auburn highlights,
❏ SUNSET	Golden or caramel brown (light, medium or dark) sometimes with copper highlights
❏ SUNLIGHT	Brown (light, medium, or dark), but I don't see myself clearly in any of the above categories; I have both warm and cool tones mixed together

Black

❏ SUNRISE	Cool, deep blue-black
❏ SUNSET	Warm, deep brown-black (no blue present)

Gray

❏ SUNRISE	Snow white, silver gray, with cool blue undertones
❏ SUNSET	Cream white, winter white, pewter white (not as blue-gray as silver)
❏ SUNLIGHT	Gray, but I don't see myself as being distinctly in any of the above categories; I'm a mixture

Sunrise Gray

Sunset Brown

Sunlight Red

Each Colortime has blondes, redheads, brunettes, and grays in varying tones. There are no black-haired people in the Sunlight Colortime.

Sunrise Olive

UNSURE OF YOUR SKIN TONE? JUST PICK THE SKIN TONE THAT IS CLOSEST TO DESCRIBING YOUR COLORING, OR ASK A FRIEND TO HELP.

What Is Your Skin Tone?

Sunset Brown

Olive (olive skin has an exotic, slightly yellow-green undertone for all three palettes)

❑ SUNRISE   Olive (light, medium, or deep) with cool green undertones
☑ SUNSET   Olive (light, medium, or deep) with warm golden undertones
❑ SUNLIGHT   Olive, but I don't think I belong in either of the above categories

Black or Brown

❑ SUNRISE   Blue-black or rosy brown
❑ SUNSET   Golden honey brown (light, medium, or dark)
❑ SUNLIGHT   Very light brown

Fair

❑ SUNRISE   Fair, cool white
❑ SUNSET   Warm, creamy white
❑ SUNLIGHT   Ivory

Beige

Sunlight Fair

❑ SUNRISE   Rose beige or rose pink
❑ SUNSET   Warm peach beige (light, medium, or deep)
❑ SUNLIGHT   Beige, but I have a mixture of both rose and peach undertones

SCORE YOUR ANSWERS TO QUESTION 4

My eye color is:	❑ SUNRISE	☒ SUNSET	❑ SUNLIGHT
My hair color is:	❑ SUNRISE	☒ SUNSET	❑ SUNLIGHT
My skin tone is:	❑ SUNRISE	☒ SUNSET	❑ SUNLIGHT

If you marked two or three in one column, this is definitely your Colortime palette. If you marked one in each Colortime palette, go with Sunlight. Sunlight is a balanced combination of Sunrise and Sunset, so it's a no-fail compromise. You may decide later that you have an emotional attachment to one palette or another and change your mind, but more about this later. Stick to Sunlight for now.

WHAT THE QUIZ MEANS

After analyzing the preferences of thousands of students, clients, and audiences, I know that the palette people choose in question 1 is likely to be the one they choose in questions 2 and 3 as well. Most people discover that the Colortime palette that includes the colors of their skin, hair, and eyes is their favorite. Your natural color sense draws you to these colors.

Just as everything in nature is designed to blend, you were born with blending skin, hair, and eye color. Study the color of Siamese cats and you will see how their eyes, fur, noses, and foot pads all blend into a particular Colortime. Look at Irish setter puppies in a pet store window—all of their golden colors fit into the Sunset palette.

Go back to question 4 to make certain that you chose the right colors for your eyes, hair, and skin tones. Check your eye color first in a good light. You may discover colors in your eyes you've never seen before. Brown-eyed people are often amazed when I point out the green in their eyes. Take the time to really study yourself. Look at the undertones in your skin and hair. That's a really interesting person with lots of colorful potential staring back at you in the mirror.

If you find it hard to be objective, ask a friend to help you. It's often easier when someone else helps you judge your coloring. If two out of the three personal colorings, such as your eyes and hair, are in one of the palettes, you can feel assured that it is your palette. If you color your hair, try to find your natural hair color on the list. People often say that they can't remember—it's been so long since they've seen it! Ask a family member, an old friend, or your hairdresser—someone who knows "for sure."

Look at the clothes in your closet. Since you do most of the choosing (assuming that someone else has not done the choosing for you), most of the colors will be in your Colortime. The colors in your home are a less accurate indication of your Colortime because other people are often involved in your choices, or because you had to work with colors that were already there when you moved in, such as carpeting or tile. But if you did the decorating and are really happy with your choices, the colors that you chose can also help you find your Colortime.

Where Your Choices Take You—More about You

If you're not happy with your current wardrobe, or you're just ready for a change, the following discussion can help you determine which Colortime to use. This may be just the time for your personal and colorful Declaration of Independence!

If you circled the same Colortime palette in answer to all four questions, you should have little trouble choosing colors because you have a really strong affinity for the particular Colortime palette that you circled—Sunrise, Sunlight, or Sunset. You will feel your absolute best when you wear and use the colors in that Colortime. That's the good news.

The bad news is that because you have this strong pull in one direction, you might be somewhat inflexible in decisions involving someone in another Colortime (husband, wife, business partner, teenage daughter, others involved in planning a wedding, and so on.). You are not, however, apt to be confused about *your* Colortime. People are likely to ask for your advice because you are so decisive—but you're likely to advise them to use your favorite colors!

What happens if you chose different palettes for questions 2 and 3? This just means that you could be content to "dress" your surroundings in a different Colortime from the one in which you dress yourself. Your clothing should reflect your personal coloring, but your home may reflect a particular mood from another Colortime. I've written another book called, *Colors for Your Every Mood*, that explains these colorful moods. You are more flexible than the person mentioned earlier who has chosen the same palette throughout, but the bad news here is that you may have difficulty making a decision because you are so flexible.

Is it possible to favor two Colortime palettes equally? The answer to that question is yes. You could probably be happy using any of the Colortime palettes you circled. You are probably delightful to work with because of your flexibility, but you may find it hard to decide which palette to use and where. Extra freedom of choice can mean extra confusion!

I often advise clients to go with their hearts, not with their heads. The color that gives you that emotional tug is the one you want to use. If you analyze and agonize too much, you lose the point of what color is all about.

With clothing choices, I feel it's best to choose the Colortime palette that contains your personal skin, hair, and eye coloring and stay with it most of the time—it's more flattering and makes you look your best. It is also more practical and easier on the budget, and everything you wear will blend well with other colors in the same Colortime. If, however, you have a really favorite color in another Colortime, there are ways to integrate that color into your wardrobe. We'll get into that later.

If you have a strong aversion to a particular Colortime, then you obviously should avoid using it because you'll be uncomfortable surrounded by these colors. You are also likely to be definite about your other dislikes.

Have you ever gotten a sweater from someone in a color that you felt looked awful on you? Chances are that it was in the giver's Colortime, not yours. The giver may have spent hours knitting it and think it's just wonderful. You can begin to solve that problem by telling everyone what your Colortime colors are. Maybe they'll take the hint the next time they give you something.

Should you experiment with a Colortime that you didn't circle? Chances are that you won't want to; but trends do tempt you. Your lifestyle may change, and your moods definitely do, so you feel the need to try something totally different.

Trends can be fun, and they can add a refreshing newness to your outfits, but you are more likely to tire quickly of trendy colors that are not in your preferred Colortime. It's risky to experiment with colors for a major purchase (like a suit) when you're investing a lot of money. Try these colors instead in a scarf or shirt, where you can change colors inexpensively, should you decide later that those trendy colors aren't really you at all. Try a different Colortime in an inexpensive piece of clothing or accessory before you invest a whole paycheck in something that may turn out to be a mistake.

Did you circle all of the Colortimes for all of the answers? You are the kind of person who says, "I love all colors!" That sounds wonderful, and you're very flexible—but somewhat fickle and definitely moody! Just like a kid in a candy store, you may want "two of those," and "three of these," and, wait a minute, another "one of those." You may be an extroverted type who likes everything. And you want everything...sometimes all in the same outfit!

If this sounds like you, there are two ways for you to avoid becoming totally uncoordinated.

1. In clothing, go with the palette that contains your personal coloring for the most flattering and organized solution. If you still feel that you want to wear all three palettes, don't combine them all in one outfit. It does mean that you'll have three separate wardrobe palettes, each of which needs blending accessories and, if you're a woman, blending makeup colors.
2. Use the Sunlight Colortime palette because it overlaps with both the Sunrise and Sunset palettes and offers you a wide, but more subtle, range of choices.

If you're still having difficulty finding your own coloring in one particular palette, or you simply cannot decide which pleases you the most, then I suggest that you also go with the Sunlight Colortime. This palette is a happy compromise, and because your own coloring is likely to be so varied that you find it difficult to determine which palette is yours, you may belong right in the middle, with the Sunlight palette.

Do Colortime choices ever change? In some people they do, in others they stay constant over a lifetime. Your coloring may change as you age. Your hair may start to gray and soften your look. Your skin may (but not always) start to pick up more yellow with age. (Think of handsome lace or cotton—not old newspapers!)

Your eyes do fade, but that can be an advantage because the undertones then begin to come through, and you can introduce these colorings into your wardrobe. You may have been born a Sunrise and loved many of this palette's bright shades as a child and young adult. But as nature ages and softens your coloring, you might want to switch to the softer Sunlight palette. Then again, your coloring may remain fairly constant, especially if you color your hair, and you may continue to wear the same colors you wore when you were younger.

Don't let the existence of many different types of coloring in each Colortime confuse you. There are light, medium, and dark colorings in each palette. All you need to do is to look at the closest description of hair, skin, and eyes in each Colortime to come up with the right combination for you.

Within racial or ethnic groups, there are many variations. All "black" skins are obviously not black, and all people of color should carefully consider undertones of their skin before picking their Colortime. Refer to question 4 in the quiz to see how each Colortime includes a variety of skin tones.

Asian skins may fall into any of the three Colortimes. Some Asians have very blue-black hair and eyes, with the cool green olive undertones of Sunrise; others have the deep but very warm hair and eye coloring and warm olive skin of Sunset. If you are of mixed racial background, you may fall into the Sunlight palette.

Ruddy or florid skins may also be found in all three palettes, so basing your choice on hair and eye color may be the best way to find out which palette is yours. For example, florid skin is typical in redheads or redheads who have gone gray. If their eyes and hair have warm undertones, even though their skin is flushed, they are in the Sunset palette.

If you're in doubt, let your initial, emotional reaction to the three palettes be your guide, and you'll find yourself in your best Colortime.

CHOICES—"RIGHT" OR "WRONG"

It is important to remember that there are no "right" or "wrong" answers to any quiz in this book. No one is going to give you a poor grade and make you stand in a colorless corner if you make the "wrong" choices.

You cannot make a mistake in choosing your Colortime palette, because Colortime choices are simply a question of personal, natural reactions. I am not placing you in a little color cubicle and telling you not to stray from it. I would never presume to tell you what your Colortime is without first asking you how you feel about certain colors. Since I can't be right there with you, the quiz stands in for me by asking the questions that I would ask.

It is interesting to me that children have no problem at all choosing colors for themselves; they are so "free" and uninhibited. But adults become very analytical and self-conscious and often choose colors because of what a friend suggests. Your friend—wonderful person that he or she may be—cannot tell you how you feel or what you see.

You may have been surprised by your responses to the quiz. Did you find yourself in a palette you would never have expected to be in? That should tell you something. Maybe it's time for a change—go for it!

2

FIND YOUR
PERFECT COLOR PALETTE

Everything in nature, including color, works on a time clock. We associate certain shadings, tints, values, and intensities with specific times of day, so it makes sense to organize colors into palettes that represent morning (Sunrise), noon (Sunlight), and evening (Sunset).

Writers and poets traditionally use colors to describe various hours. Dawn is apt to be either "rosy" or "cold and gray," Sunshine is invariably yellow, and cowboys always ride off into a "blazing golden sunset!"

INSPIRATION OF THE IMPRESSIONISTS

The Impressionist painters transformed art history with their efforts to capture the full impression of nature and the play of light on a particular scene at a particular time. Claude Monet, renowned for his magical studies of water lilies, often painted the same subject to show how its colors varied at different times of the day.

Colors do appear to vary during the course of a day because of changing light and the presence of various particles that float in the atmosphere. Look at the illustrations of the Colortimes to see what I mean. Throughout the text, you will note that Sunrise is also called "AM"; Sunset, "PM"; and Sunlight, "Midday."

THE COLORTIME PALETTES

In the earliest hours of the day, warm color begins to emerge from the cold, gray dawn. A rosy glow appears before the dazzling sun actually begins its ascent. Because sunrise is sunset in reverse, the shadings progress from the darkness of blue and gray to purpled rose-mauves to the splendor of the red-orange glow. But because the atmosphere is generally cleaner and moister in the morning, the colors of sunrise are much less fiery than those of sunset. This dewy "wetness" permeates the Sunrise Colortime.

Occasionally, when the air is very clean, there is a clear green streak across the sky just after the dawn breaks. Later in the morning, the sun changes to a brilliant yellow-white. Blues are brightest in the early hours and the sky is at its clearest. An undertone of cool blue pervades most of the Sunrise (AM) Colortime.

In the afternoon, you see the Sunset (PM) colors. The number of yellowed dust particles in the atmosphere increases at this time of day, so most colors appear to take on a golden, hazy, or mellow quality. Colors appear "drier" in the afternoon than they do in the morning. In the late afternoon, as the sun goes down, you see the fiery shades of sunset. Gold is the pervading undertone of sunset's orange, rust, warm reds, and yellow-greens. At dusk, the spectral rays of deep blue take over, often combining with the reflected reds to become a red-violet glow.

In the very middle of the clock, between 10 a.m. and 2 p.m., is the Sunlight (Midday) Colortime palette. The intensity of the sun is greatest during these hours. Even when the sun is obscured by clouds, the force of its reflected light remains strong. Any object that receives direct sunlight during these hours seems slightly diminished, because intense light dazzles the eye and makes the colors appear somewhat muted.

Since the Midday Colortime is derived from both the AM and PM palettes, it offers the widest range of choices, but the colors are subtle—they never scream. This is the palette of pleasing, luscious tones of every hue. Any of the tints may be deepened to a darker value for contrast.

Charcoal, black, and navy blue represent the shades of night and predawn, when all colors are shrouded in darkness. They may be used with all of the Colortime palettes. They are part of "Nature's Crossover Colors" and are explained more fully later in this chapter. The Crossover Colors are part of every palette.

Every color in the spectrum is represented throughout the daytime hours, although the undertones, intensities, and values vary in each Colortime palette. For example, because of its intense heat, vibrant orange doesn't appear in the Sunrise palette. The warm pinky-coral tones, such as Confetti, "stand in" for their fiery sisters. Similarly, Peaches N' Cream would do the same in the Sunlight palette.

The Colortime Quiz helped you to identify your Colortime preference. Now let's look at the colors that will work for you.

WHICH COLORTIME ARE YOU? SUNLIGHT? SUNSET? SUNRISE?

17

CERISE PANTONE® 19-1955	BRIGHT ROSE PANTONE® 18-1945	VERY BERRY PANTONE® 18-2336	SHOCKING PINK PANTONE® 17-2127	SACHET PINK PANTONE® 15-2216
ALMOND BLOSSOM PANTONE® 13-2006	PINK ICING PANTONE® 15-1717	SEA PINK PANTONE® 15-1912	GOSSAMER PINK PANTONE® 13-1513	CONFETTI PANTONE® 16-1723
BLUSHING BRIDE PANTONE® 12-1310	RASPBERRY RADIANCE PANTONE® 19-2432	VIVID VIOLA PANTONE® 18-3339	SPARKLING GRAPE PANTONE® 19-3336	AMETHYST ORCHID PANTONE® 17-3628
LAVENDER PANTONE® 15-3817	VIOLET TULLE PANTONE® 16-3416	CYCLAMEN PANTONE® 16-3118	IBIS ROSE PANTONE® 17-2520	PRISM PINK PANTONE® 14-2311
LILAC SNOW PANTONE® 13-3405	GRAPE ROYALE PANTONE® 19-3518	PRISM VIOLET PANTONE® 19-3748	BLUE IRIS PANTONE® 18-3943	PERSIAN JEWEL PANTONE® 17-3934
VISTA BLUE PANTONE® 15-3930	DEEP ULTRAMARINE PANTONE® 19-3950	SNORKEL BLUE PANTONE® 19-4049	PALACE BLUE PANTONE® 18-4043	LITTLE BOY BLUE PANTONE® 16-4132
BLUE BELL PANTONE® 14-4121	BONNIE BLUE PANTONE® 16-4134	BLUE JEWEL PANTONE® 18-4535	BLUE ATOLL PANTONE® 16-4535	CAPRI BREEZE PANTONE® 17-4735
CERAMIC PANTONE® 16-5127	BEACH GLASS PANTONE® 13-5412	EMERALD PANTONE® 17-5641	ELECTRIC GREEN PANTONE® 14-5721	SPRING BOUQUET PANTONE® 14-6340
DAIQUIRI GREEN PANTONE® 12-0435	BUTTERFLY PANTONE® 12-0322	CHARDONNAY PANTONE® 13-0633	GLACIER GRAY PANTONE® 14-4102	FROST GRAY PANTONE® 17-0000
LILAC MARBLE PANTONE® 14-3903	GRAY DAWN PANTONE® 14-4106	BRIGHT WHITE PANTONE® 11-0601	DEEP MAHOGANY PANTONE® 19-1420	SPHINX PANTONE® 16-1703

SUNRISE COLORS

PHOTO: GREG BOYD

EYES

- Pure blue, cool clear light blue, medium blue, or blue-gray
- Rosy brown (light, medium, or dark)
- Very dark brown, almost jet black
- Gray hazel (a combination of blue, gray, and perhaps some green)
- Bright blue-green

SKIN

- Olive (light, medium, or deep) with cool green undertones
- Blue-black or rosy brown
- Fair, cool white
- Rose beige or rose pink

HAIR

- Ash or sandy blonde (light, medium or dark)
- Platinum blonde or towhead Auburn, with cool blue undertones
- Ash brown (light, medium or dark, but without gold)
- Dark brown, may have auburn highlights
- Cool, deep blue-black
- Snow white
- Silver gray, with cool blue undertones

ABOUT SUNRISES

The Sunrise (A.M.) Colortime is the palette of the natural elements of air and water—transparent and frosty with predominantly cool blue undertones. Yet as the dazzling sun begins its ascent, the shadings progress from the darkness of blue and gray, purpled rose-mauves and vibrant pinks, to the splendor of the red-orange glow, less fiery than the sunset in the clear, dewy, freshness of morning.

Your palette literally sparkles, and many of your colors are such "jewel" and "royal" tones as Amethyst Orchid, Grape Royale, Palace Blue, Emerald, Blue Jewel, and Prism Pink. Your warm colors are pure and cooled down Pink Icing, Sea Pink, and Chardonnay. Your yellow-greens are fresh, clean, and bright Electric Green, Spring Bouquet, and Butterfly. Your blues and blue-greens are crisp and cool and promise a tropical destination, like Snorkel Blue and Capri Breeze.

Use orange and red-orange sparingly as accents. They may be lightened to warm pinkish confetti tones or deepened to rich mahogany browns, just as nature does in the short span of sunrise. Cool grays, rose-beiges, and mauvy-taupes are natural neutrals for your palette. Your best white is pure-as-the-driven-snow white.

THE SUNRISE (AM) COLORTIME PALETTE

If you chose the Sunrise palette, the natural elements of water and air are a strong influence on the predominantly cool blue undertones of your Colortime palette.

Your palette literally sparkles, and many of your colors are such "jewel" and "royal" tones as:

| AMETHYST ORCHID | GRAPE ROYALE | PALACE BLUE | EMERALD |
| BLUE JEWEL | PRISM PINK | SPARKLING GRAPE | |

The cool colors are often transparent and frosty:

| LILAC SNOW | BEACH GLASS | DAIQUIRI GREEN | GLACIER GRAY |

The warm colors in your palette are pure and cooled down:

| PINK ICING | SEA PINK | CHARDONNAY | VERY BERRY |

The yellow-greens of the Sunrise are fresh, clean, and bright, as in glowing, iridescent butterfly wings or the new green growth found in springtime:

| ELECTRIC GREEN | SPRING BOUQUET | BUTTERFLY |

The blues and blue-greens are crisp and cool and promise a tropical destination:

| SNORKEL BLUE | CAPRI BREEZE | ULTRAMARINE BLUE | BLUE ATOLL |

Orange and red-orange play a very small role in your Colortime and are usually least favored by people who choose this palette. If you should borrow them from the Sunset palette, use them sparingly as accents, just as nature does in the short span of sunrise. Oranges work best for you when you lighten them to warm pinkish tones or deepen them to rich mahogany browns.

Cool grays, rose-beiges, and mauvy-taupes are natural neutrals for your palette.

The best white for Sunrises is pure-as-the-driven-snow white.

THE SUNSET (PM) COLORTIME PALETTE

If you chose the Sunset palette, you prefer the natural elements of fire and earth of the Sunset (PM) palette that light up your predominantly golden undertones.

You'll have fun with Fiesta Red and Bright Chartreuse, and you'll literally light up the sky with Deep Periwinkle and Magenta Haze.

When it's time to cool down, try a bit of Celestial, Della Robbia, Moonlight Blue, or blue-greens like Fir and Feldspar.

The colors you should use most sparingly are icy, cool, and almost transparent. They're too cold for you and will melt in the presence of your warm coloring.

Your best whites are creamy or a bit warmer than pure white.

Your palette is primarily warm and is often described as "earthy." The warm, spicy shades are important to you.

CAYENNE	GINGER	SAUTERNE	EARTH RED
TERRA COTTA			

But you should not be so "down-to-earth," however, that you do not enjoy a touch of the exotic:

BOUGAINVILLEA	BYZANTIUM	IRIS ORCHID	MOROCCAN BLUE
MIMOSA			

These greens can give special flavor to your life:

PESTO	CORIANDER

Your taste can also be tempted with the sweet shades of:

HONEY GOLD	APRICOT CREAM	LATTÉ	CRANBERRY
HOT CHOCOLATE			

Other earth colors that are important to this Colortime are:

CADMIUM ORANGE	AMBER YELLOW	MUTED CLAY	CAMEL

You're happier in coral pink tones, such as:

SUNKIST CORAL	BURNT CORAL	LIVING CORAL

FIESTA PANTONE® 17-1564	CRANBERRY PANTONE® 17-1545	CAYENNE PANTONE® 18-1651	TIGERLILY PANTONE® 17-1456	EARTH RED PANTONE® 18-1631
GiNGER PANTONE® 17-1444	SUNKIST CORAL PANTONE® 17-1736	BURNT CORAL PANTONE® 16-1529	LIVING CORAL PANTONE® 16-1546	CADMIUM ORANGE PANTONE® 15-1340
PEACH PANTONE® 14-1227	BELLINI PANTONE® 13-1114	MUTED CLAY PANTONE® 16-1330	TERRA COTTA PANTONE® 16-1526	DEEP PERIWINKLE PANTONE® 17-3932
BOUGAINVILLEA PANTONE® 17-3725	MOONLITE MAUVE PANTONE® 16-2614	IRIS ORCHID PANTONE® 17-3323	MAGENTA HAZE PANTONE® 18-2525	BYZANTIUM PANTONE® 19-3138
MOROCCAN BLUE PANTONE® 19-4241	DELLA ROBBIA BLUE PANTONE® 16-4020	CELESTIAL PANTONE® 18-4530	MOONLIGHT BLUE PANTONE® 18-4027	DEEP PEACOCK BLUE PANTONE® 17-5029

SUNSET COLORS

GREEN MOSS PANTONE® 17-0636	PESTO PANTONE® 18-0228	FERN PANTONE® 16-0430	BRIGHT CHARTREUSE PANTONE® 14-0445	SAUTERNE PANTONE® 15-0942
PAMPAS PANTONE® 14-0826	FIR PANTONE® 18-5621	FELDSPAR PANTONE® 16-5815	AMBER YELLOW PANTONE® 13-0942	MIMOSA PANTONE® 14-0848
HONEY GOLD PANTONE® 15-1142	APRICOT CREAM PANTONE® 13-1027	WARM TAUPE PANTONE® 16-1318	COGNAC PANTONE® 18-1421	HOT CHOCOLATE PANTONE® 19-1325
CAMEL PANTONE® 17-1224	CARAMEL PANTONE® 16-1439	DOE PANTONE® 16-1333	LATTÉ PANTONE® 15-1220	WINTER WHEAT PANTONE® 14-1119
WINTER WHITE PANTONE® 11-0507	TAUPE GRAY PANTONE® 17-0808	CHATEAU GRAY PANTONE® 15-4503	CORIANDER PANTONE® 17-1113	SEPIA PANTONE® 18-0928

EYES

- Mid or deep blue (often with warm flecks of color)
- Amber, warm golden brown (light, medium, or dark)
- Golden hazel (a combination of brown, gold, green, and perhaps some blue)
- Green with golden flecks

SKIN

- Olive (light, medium, or deep) with warm golden undertones
- Golden honey brown (light, medium, or dark)
- Warm, creamy white
- Warm peach beige (light, medium, or deep)

ABOUT SUNSETS

The elements of fire and earth underscore the Sunset (PM) palette and speak of a mellowed, golden evening. Warm tones prevail, as they light up your predominantly golden undertones. The warm, spicy shades are important to you, with a touch of the exotic. Your greens like Pesto and Coriander add special flavor to your life. Your taste can also be tempted with the sweet shades of Honey Gold, Apricot Cream, Cranberry, and Hot Chocolate. Other earth colors that are important to you include Cadmium Orange, Amber Yellow, Muted Clay, and Camel. You're happier in coral pink tones, like Sunkist Coral, Burnt Coral, and Living Coral.

Have fun with Fiesta Red and Bright Chartreuse, and light up the sky with Deep Periwinkle and Magenta Haze. When it's time to cool down, try a bit of Celestial, Della Robbia, Moonlight Blue, or blue-greens like Fir and Feldspar.

The colors you should use most sparingly are icy, cool, and almost transparent. They're too cold for you and will melt in the presence of your warm coloring.

Your best whites are creamy or a bit warmer than pure white.

HAIR

- Golden, honey, or coppery blonde (light, medium or dark)
- Golden copper red (light, medium, or dark)
- Rust-wine red, like Bordeaux
- Golden or caramel brown (light, medium or dark) sometimes with copper highlights

QUE ROSE TONE® 18-1634	DESERT ROSE PANTONE® 17-1927	PEONY PANTONE® 15-1816	WILD ROSE PANTONE® 16-1715	BLUSH PANTONE® 15-1614
DER PINK TONE 14-1511	CAMEO PINK PANTONE® 14-2307	MAUVE MIST PANTONE® 15-3207	DUSTY LAVENDER PANTONE® 17-3313	RED VIOLET PANTONE® 17-1818
E NECTAR TONE 18-1710	PURPLE HAZE PANTONE 16-3718	VIOLA PANTONE® 16-3815	NIRVANA PANTONE® 17-3808	PLACID BLUE PANTONE® 15-3920
ER LAKE BLUE TONE® 17-4030	CORNFLOWER BLUE PANTONE® 16-4031	DELFT PANTONE® 19-4039	INFINITY PANTONE® 17-4015	CENDRE BLUE PANTONE® 17-4131
E TURQUOISE TONE® 15-5217	PETIT FOUR PANTONE® 14-4516	NILE BLUE PANTONE® 15-5210	VERDANT GREEN PANTONE® 19-6026	JADEITE PANTONE® 16-5304

SUNLIGHT COLORS

GREEN TONE® 15-6316	BERYL GREEN PANTONE® 16-5515	WEEPING WILLOW PANTONE® 15-0525	WINTER PEAR PANTONE® 15-0523	LINDEN GREEN PANTONE® 15-0533
EO GREEN TONE® 14-6312	CUSTARD PANTONE® 13-0720	CORNSILK PANTONE® 13-0932	JOJOBA PANTONE® 14-0935	SUNBURST PANTONE® 13-1030
CHES N' CREAM TONE® 14-1521	PEACH PARFAIT PANTONE® 14-1219	BISQUE PANTONE® 13-1109	DEEP TAUPE PANTONE® 18-1312	WOODROSE PANTONE® 16-1806
LWOOD TONE® 17-1516	ROSE DUST PANTONE® 14-1307	MELLOW BUFF PANTONE® 13-1014	PEARLED IVORY PANTONE® 11-0907	WHISPER WHITE PANTONE® 11-0701
EN HAZE TONE® 14-0615	CLOUD GRAY PANTONE® 15-3802	MOONSTRUCK PANTONE® 14-4500	MIRAGE GRAY PANTONE® 15-4703	SIMPLY TAUPE PANTONE® 16-0906

EYES

- Blue, but somewhat changeable depending on the color you are wearing
- Brown, but often flecked with a combination of several colors
- Hazel, but subject to change with colors you are wearing
- Light or medium blue-green

SKIN

- Olive (light to medium)
- Very light brown
- Ivory
- Beige, but with a mixture of both rose and peach undertones

ABOUT SUNLIGHTS

The Sunlight (Midday) Colortime is the palette of the luscious sun-drenched noon hours. Colors of all the natural elements of air, water, fire and earth are softened and slightly muted by the intensity of the sun—never paled, just muted. This is the palette of the luscious tones of ice cream, sherbet, gelato, Grape Nectar, Peaches N' Cream, and Custard. Your best blues are cool Cornflower Blue, Silver Lake Blue, and Placid Blue. Romantic roses really become you—from deeper, more sensuous Baroque Rose and Desert Rose, to soft yet sophisticated Woodrose and Rose Dust, to nostalgic Cameo Pink and Powder Pink. Your purples are not shrinking violets, they're Viola and Red Violet. Your greens and blue-greens are lovely mineral Jadeite, Beryl Green, and Blue Turquoise. Avoid overly bright colors except as an added touch. Crossover True Red is the best of your brights, while deeper tones of Verdant Green and Infinity Blue, Deep Taupe, and Burlwood provide contrast.

Simply Taupe, Moonstruck, and the Crossover neutrals combine well with both your warm and the cool hues. Your best white is a quiet Whisper White or a not-quite-white with pastel undertones like Pearled Ivory.

HAIR

- Blonde (light, medium, or dark), but a mixture of both warm and cool blonde tones
- Red, mixed with both warm and cool tones
- Brown (light, medium, or dark) with both warm and cool tones
- Gray, in a mixture of warm and cool

Colortime Concepts™ from *More Alive with Color* © 2006 by Leatrice Eiseman: www.colorexpert.com

THE SUNLIGHT (MIDDAY) COLORTIME PALETTE

If you chose the Sunlight palette, your Colortime dips into both Sunrise and Sunset, but very selectively. Yours are the softened, muted, sun-drenched tints. They are more intense and interesting than pale pastels, never "wishy-washy" or nondescript.

Any of the natural elements of air, water, fire, and earth are present in your palette, but they are never flamboyant. The hot shades of Sunset would overwhelm this palette, but a Peony pink is perfect. The Prism Violet of Sunrise would work better if gentled to the muted tones of Purple Haze

Many of the tints and shadings are those of delicious ice cream, sherbet, gelato, and flavored yogurt. These confection colors are really yummy on you. In fact, many of your hues are truly delectable:

GRAPE NECTAR	WINTER PEAR	PETIT FOUR	PEACHES N' CREAM
PEACH PARFAIT	CUSTARD	BISQUE	

The colors of the plates on which you might serve your food describe some of your best blues:

DELFT	CORNFLOWER BLUE	SILVER LAKE BLUE	PLACID BLUE

Roses are really special on you. They're romantic and appealing in a variety of undertones: deeper and more sensuous red roses like Baroque Rose and Desert Rose, sophisticated and soft Woodrose and Rose Dust. Others are nostalgic, like Cameo Pink and Powder Pink.

The purples are not shrinking violets, especially in Viola and Red Violet.

Many of the greens and blue-greens are lovely mineral shades, like Jadeite, Beryl Green, and Blue Turquoise.

Subtle is a key word for Midday palettes. If given a choice, opt for the subtle. Avoid overly bright colors; they won't work as well for you and are best used as an added touch. Crossover True Red is the best of the brights for Midday as everyone needs at least a touch of red, especially for holidays and special occasions. (Learn more about the Crossover Colors on page 30.) Fiery orange is not a good choice for this palette. Lighten it to Peach Parfait or a sunny shade of Sunburst and you'll be much happier with it.

As contrast is important in any palette of colors, there are some deeper tones included in this Colortime. There are, for example, Verdant Green and Infinity Blue, Deep Taupe, Burlwood, and for a really restful lavender, there is zenlike Nirvana.

Neutral tones such as Simply Taupe and Moonstruck, in addition to the Crossover neutrals, combine well with both the warm and the cool hues of your Colortime; and since neutrals are never noisy, they will also work best for you.

Your best white is a quiet Whisper White. A-not-quite-white with pastel undertones like Pearled Ivory is also good.

WHAT COLOR CAN DO FOR YOU

Color has enormous influence in your life, starting from the day you were first able to discern the colors in the world around you.

Color can direct and divert the eye, communicate emotion, create moods and optical illusions, delight, or add dignity. It has enormous influence in your life, starting from the day you were first able to discern the colors in the world around you.

Nature's paint box yields wonderful possibilities. There are limitless tints or tones to excite you or calm you, elate you or depress you, warm you or cool you. Color may heighten your awareness and make you more sensitive to your surroundings.

Color can enhance your self-image as well and make you feel marvelous. I have seen some amazing changes when people find their personal palettes. One of the first messages you give to other people before you ever say a word is communicated in the colors you use. Haven't you seen someone in a magazine or on the street and thought, "I wish I could get myself together like that!" You can look just as good (or even better) when you learn to use your "personal colors." Color is the key to getting that look.

An "Eye" for Color

Is an "eye" for color like an "ear" for music? Are we born with a sense of color? I think both of these questions can be answered yes and no. Some experts feel that we may be predisposed to certain abilities through artistic ancestors, whereas others believe an "eye" for color can be learned.

You don't have to be born a child prodigy to play the piano. Through instruction and practice you can learn to play well enough to satisfy your needs. You may never perform like a rock star or a concert pianist, but you can still get a sense of satisfaction and enjoyment out of playing.

The same holds true for color. You may not have been born with artistic ability, but you can learn how to use color so it works wonders for you and gives you tremendous satisfaction. When you arrange flowers in a vase, take a photograph, put an outfit together, choose the right shade of lipstick, or serve food on a plate, you are the artist.

Affinity and Attraction

- **Af-fin-i-ty:** The relatioship existing between persons or things that are naturally or involuntarily drawn together.
- **At-trac-tion:** To draw by appeal to natural or excited interest, emotion, or esthetic sense.

You have a natural affinity for or attraction to certain colors and Colortimes. When you walk by a flower shop and see many beautiful arrangements, one or two will catch your eye. There may be a large selection to choose from, but some are more special to you than others. Texture, scent, and design will also attract you, but color often draws your attention first.

What you see pleases your esthetic sense—your appreciation of beauty. Some of the bouquets are so special to you that they almost take your breath away. You are attracted to certain colors because they are in tune with your natural Colortime preferences.

AF-FIN-I-TY: THE RELATIONSHIP BETWEEN PERSONS OR THINGS THAT ARE NATURALLY OR INVOLUNTARILY DRAWN TOGETHER.

What You Feel

Catalogs, websites, magazines, and store displays often show great-looking clothes or a beautifully made up model. Maybe you can even see yourself, magically transformed, in a special outfit. There is something irresistible then that tugs at you and appeals to your emotions. What you feel pleases you.

One of my former students just loved beige and brown, but she felt she was in a color rut. Why did those colors feel so natural to her? When we got into a discussion about these colors, we discovered that her school uniform had been beige and brown. Although many people might turn away from the colors they had to wear for years (such as Army fatigue green), she had pleasant memories—she adored her school years and remembered them as the happiest time of her life. She was a good student who felt a sense of accomplishment and was secure and popular. I told her that if browns and beiges made her feel all of those good things, she should continue to use them, but I suggested she add a "pop" of color, especially near her face, to alleviate the "same-old, same-old" look and add variety to her wardrobe—and her life.

If the same colors continue to make you happy over the years, there's no need to switch. Often a touch of an interesting accent color is all that is necessary for a new look. I suggested touches of Cayenne and Mimosa from her PM Colortime palette to add some zest to the earth tones.

Many people make the mistake of switching to "new" colors simply because of the novelty. They soon grow tired of their selections and realize they never felt quite comfortable in that piece of clothing.

Remember that each Colortime palette has both warm and cool colors, plus light, medium, and dark values of each of them, so there is enormous flexibility within each palette. If you have a really strong affinity for a certain Colortime, you never have to leave it. You can stay completely within the framework of your own Colortime and still achieve the necessary variety. As a matter of fact, it's important to maintain a balance between warm and cool colors, regardless of the Colortime you have selected.

ALWAYS BALANCE YOUR WARM AND COOL COLORS

COLOR YOUR THINKING

At this point, you may be thinking, "If I have this natural affinity, why is it that I may not be happy with my color choices?" There are several explanations:

1. You allow too many outside influences to color your thinking (pun intended). These can include family, friends, fads, persuasive advertising, and the bargains you find so hard to resist. Bargains may be marvelous for the budget, but the bargain that sits forgotten in the closet is no bargain. Have you ever been given a gift like a sweater and had to pretend that you loved it? Or put on a jazzy hat and felt that you had contracted instant yellow jaundice when you saw it reflected next to your face in the mirror? Chances are that the color you chose (or that someone else chose for you) was not in your personal Colortime. Do you often give people gifts in the colors you like best? They probably do the same to you! Now you can let everyone know what your Colortime is, and you can learn to choose colors that will please everyone on your gift list. This will save you money by helping you to avoid expensive mistakes.

2. Colors are rarely used in isolation. Choosing one color that you really like may be simple for you. But combining that hue with other shades, tints, and intensities can be troublesome. Don't let finding the correct combination deadlock your efforts. If this is the part that confuses you, read on. The "how tos" and how they work are in the next chapter.

3. The psychological and emotional impacts of color can delight you or devastate you. It is almost impossible to separate the "seeing" of color from the "feeling," because so much of what you see is based on what you feel. Colors evoke emotions—some pleasant, some very unpleasant. You can be turned off to a terrific color because of some experience long past.

Does pink make you think of the first prom corsage you ever got (or gave) or does it remind you of the time that you ate too much cotton candy at a carnival and got sick on the way home? Personal experience definitely influences your reaction to a particular color. Certain colors and color combinations can put that wondrous tape recorder in your head on "instant rewind." You never really forget anything you have ever learned; you just deposit it in your memory bank for future withdrawals.

Keeping an Open Mind

Even though you may respond favorably to most colors in your Colortime, there may be some color you don't like because of a negative experience you associate with that particular shade. Most of the time you can't even remember why. Consider the following story:

While I was doing "personal colors" for one of my clients, she told me that her husband was encouraging her to "use more purple." That instantly told me that her husband was highly creative, and it turned out he was an artist.

She, on the other hand, had a really hard time with anything remotely purple, particularly lavender. I asked her to try to remember why she might be having such a difficult time. She thought about it for several days and then recalled that as a child she'd had a wonderful loving relationship with her grandmother. She often brought her sprigs of lavender, since it was her grandmother's favorite color. The grandmother had beautiful Sunrise silver hair and wore the color a great deal. She also loved touches of lavender throughout the house in delicate potpourris.

When my client was eight, her beloved grandmother died. Of course, she was buried in a lavender dress and everyone sent various shades of purple flowers to the funeral.

I had all the clues I needed to understand why she was so turned off by those colors. This had been her first experience with death, and she was so traumatized by it that she simply locked the painful event away in her subconscious. The memories of that difficult day faded, but her grandmother's favorite color had become associated with a deep sense of loss.

When my client asked for my help in overcoming her purple prejudice, I gave her the same advice I give to anyone who really wants to become open to trying new colors: for every negative experience, find a positive flip side of pleasurable associations. In this particular case, once the client remembered the unpleasant associations, she could deal with them and turn to the happier aspects.

There is a delightful postscript to this story. For her daughter's wedding, the mother of the bride chose (you guessed it) a lavender dress. When I called to congratulate her on her daughter's marriage, she thanked me profusely for opening her up to purple. Now when she looks in the bedroom mirror and sees herself surrounded by lavender accents, she realizes how much like her grandmother she has become (her AM palette is the same) and what marvelous stories she will be able to tell her own grandchildren.

If she hadn't allowed herself to experience the color, those important years with her grandmother might have remained hidden forever. Few of us have such poignant stories to relate, but we all need to keep an open mind to color. You never know when you might unwrap a beautiful box of memories—all in living color. Think about this story when you plan your own wedding!

Another of my clients, a multitalented artist, author, and screenwriter, loves white—anything and everything in white, especially gardenias. When I asked her if she knew why she was so in love with the color, she only had to think for a moment to remember "two of my favorite people: my great grandmother and my grandmother. My ninety-seven-year-old great grandmother had gorgeous white hair, fair skin, and an adorable smile. I remember walking with her as a very small girl of six or seven with her little dog, on snowy days in Montreal, to the movies ... the three movie buffs—pooch included—off together." She continued, "My grandmother was also very beautiful—white hair and a dynamic sense of humor—and I was mad about her. The white-white of the gardenia with its sweet fragrance reminds me of those two marvelous ladies."

This client still loves white, which is especially flattering to her own clear, fair complexion. You may not think you're always aware of color, but you truly are.

COLOR'S MESSAGE MAY BE SUBLIMINAL, BUT IT'S ALWAYS THERE TO CREATE AN EFFECT AND TO COLOR YOUR DECISIONS, YOUR MOODS, AND YOUR WORLD.

THE CROSSOVERS–NATURE'S MOST VERSATILE COLORS

The Crossovers may be used with all of the Colortime palettes. They're often used as background colors, either in combination with other colors or in the same way a neutral color might be used.

Certain colors on my Color Clock I call "Crossover Colors." Because these colors occur most frequently in nature, your eye is accustomed to seeing them in combination with many other colors.

How can you take advantage of Mother Nature's favorite background colors? Use them in the background of a print, in stripes, or as accessory colors.

THE CROSSOVERS

TRUE RED
PANTONE® 19-1664

BEAUJOLAIS
PANTONE® 18-2027

EGGPLANT
PANTONE® 19-2311

NAVY BLUE
PANTONE® 19-3832

FADED DENIM
PANTONE® 17-4021

SKY BLUE
PANTONE® 14-4318

SEAGRASS
PANTONE® 16-6008

PINENEEDLE
PANTONE® 19-5920

TEAL
PANTONE® 17-4919

CHARCOAL GRAY
PANTONE® 18-0601

NEUTRAL GRAY
PANTONE® 17-4402

JET BLACK
PANTONE® 19-0303

CAPPUCCINO
PANTONE® 19-1220

DARK EARTH
PANTONE® 19-1020

LIGHT TAUPE
PANTONE® 16-1210

PALE KHAKI
PANTONE® 15-1216

BLEACHED SAND
PANTONE® 13-1008

SUNLIGHT
PANTONE® 13-0822

SKY BLUE

Sky Blue can bring a cooling, balancing touch to contrasting warm tones, especially on a hot summer day. Did you ever look at a red geranium, a purple iris, or a yellow daffodil against the backdrop of a blue sky and think, "What an awful color combination ... Mother Nature really goofed!" Of course not. We're aware of the blue of the sky around us nearly every day. Blue skies far outnumber cloudy (or smoggy) days in most climates. As a result, our eyes and minds are accustomed to a blue backdrop for nature's myriad colors.

FADED DENIM

Is there anyone who would deny that a great pair of jeans can go almost anywhere? Obviously, there are many shades of blue jeans, but Faded Denim best describes the color of that basic, multi-purpose piece of clothing in our closets.

PINENEEDLE

Would you banish a fern from your living room because it clashed with the sofa? When nature "arranges" flowers, green is the one color that appears in virtually every composition. Nature's greens are among the most versatile of hues, especially in a print or pattern. When we're outdoors we're surrounded by green plants, trees, shrubs, and grass. Even in the midst of winter snows, faithful pine trees soften the stark landscape with their graceful branches of green.

SEAGRASS

Another of nature's neutral greens, Seagrass, lightly touched with gray, provides a subtle background to a vast variety of colors. Used alone, it is a versatile shade that offers another option to the wardrobe basics.

SUNLIGHT

The clear yellow of sunlight permeates our atmosphere. Sunlight yellow works well as an engaging, cheerful color that gives a touch of warmth to cool shades that feel a little chilly. Sunlight yellow is shared by all Colortime palettes.

DARK EARTH

The varying earth tones associated with soil, tree bark, and woody plants are an integral part of nature's basic color scheme. Your eye is accustomed to these unobtrusive colors, which function marvelously well as neutral colors.

CAPPUCCINO

Another variation on the brown family, Cappuccino is a bit warmer than Dark Earth. It is more elegant than earthy, a rich and robust brown that adds flavor to many other shades, a surprisingly sophisticated shade (think mink and sable).

BEAUJOLAIS (WINE)

A classically stirring and stylish color, this deeper, delicious, full-bodied red mimics the colors of the berries and grapes that render it.

EGGPLANT (AUBERGINE)

More plum-colored than wine, Eggplant, often called Aubergine, is considered a classic in the world of fashion.

LIGHT TAUPE　　　**BLEACHED SAND**

Ideal neutrals, these are variations of taupe and beige, the colors of sand and stone. There is no end to the versatility of these balanced neutrals. They are wonderful when-in-doubt colors that work equally well with warm and cool undertones, especially in accessories and as part of a basic wardrobe.

PALE KHAKI

Inspired by natural elements, Pale Khaki is another basic neutral, an organic shade that introduces a hint of green, nature's most abundant neutral. It's not only a summertime classic, but also a color that has become a vital part of the casual or business wardrobe.

NEUTRAL GRAY

Another ideal neutral, this shade of gray is an excellent "blender." In the context of nature, gray appears subtly at dawn and dusk, often as an undertone to the blue sky, or at any time of day as the actual color of the sky when it is overcast. Since gray days are less cheery than blue days, we often feel we need to add a touch of vivid accent to brighten the gray mood.

CHARCOAL GRAY

The deepest, most powerful of the gray family, charcoal is sturdy, reliable, and strong, a very important power color.

NAVY BLUE

The color of the sky as it descends into night, Navy Blue is associated with the strength and power of black, yet is less mysterious. It is a familiar background color and the most universal of all basic colors.

JET BLACK

Just as night always follows day, black is the inevitable shade. Its protective cover brings both strength and power as we are comforted by the respite of night, intrigued by the prospect of what the darkness might hold, and fascinated by its mystery. Jet Black is the quintessential basic color, offering a sophisticated backdrop to all other colors.

TRUE RED

Think about the frequency of red in nature and how it has been used as a signal color in natural settings. True Red is the most versatile of reds; it gives life to both warm and cool colors.

TEAL

The undulating color of a tropical sea awash with both warm and cool currents, Teal is unique—versatile and flattering to all skin types.

INTIMATE ENVIRONMENTS AND EXTENDED ENVIRONMENTS

Of the many environments that surround you, that of your clothing and cosmetics is the most personal. It is called your "intimate environment." You choose clothing and cosmetic colors just as you do anything else in your environment, because you have an affinity for those colors and because they create a pleasing and comfortable atmosphere around you.

Your esthetic color sense—what you see—plays an important role in your wardrobe decisions, especially in terms of what you see in the mirror. If you have hair the color of burnished copper, one glance in the looking glass tells you how smashing you look in bronzes and peaches. And if your skin is sallow, no one should have to tell you to avoid chartreuse.

You may have really good "instincts" about your personal colors. You have learned how to read the reactions of others, and you know when your choices are validated by a favorable comment—or no comment at all. You can train your eye to quickly recognize flattering or unflattering personal colors. Let your Colortime Quiz be your guide. If you have any doubts at all, choose your clothing colors from the Colortime that contains the colors of your skin, eyes, and hair. You will feel best when you look your best, and you will look your best when you feel your best ... it is a completed circle.

One of the most compelling reasons for doing your wardrobe in your preferred Colortime is that all of your clothing will blend and harmonize. As you have learned, you don't judge color just by what you see, you also judge it by what you feel. The feeling part is very important and cannot be ignored. I could tell you until I'm blue in the face that your best color is yellow-green because your eyes are yellow-green. But if you immediately associate an unpleasant experience with yellow-green, you will reject my suggestion no matter what I say. I might be able to convince you otherwise, but your initial reaction will remain negative.

On the other hand, your initial reaction might be very positive. If Janet and Jamie have big, beautiful blue eyes, naturally Mommie dresses Janet and Jamie in blue. Every time they wear something blue, someone comments, "Oh, look, aren't those twins adorable in their matching blue sweaters? Don't they have beautiful blue eyes!"

So Janet and Jamie get compliments, approval, and "warm fuzzies" whenever they wear blue, and it feels good. Every time they look at something that is a Midday blue (the color of their eyes), a little bell rings in their internal tape recorders, signaling approval.

Their positive response to blue is reinforced by their awareness that blue skies mean they can go outside to play. Even as adults, the twins continue to respond to blue with pleasant feelings. (You'll learn more about your color associations in the second part of this book.)

From a purely practical standpoint, you want to be sure of your color choices, because putting a wardrobe together, coloring your hair, and co-ordinating cosmetics can be an expensive proposition, and you want to get it right with the least amount of effort. As much fun as shopping can be, especially with a friend, it does take time, and that can be the biggest problem. When you shop with your own Colortime in mind, you save time because you can zero in on your best shades immediately. In addition, understanding the Color Clock will help you to increase your confidence and open your mind to exciting new color possibilities and combinations.

UNDERSTANDING UNDERTONES

To better understand the differences in the Colortime palettes, think in terms of undertone. There are both warm and cool colors in all three palettes. Warm AM colors have an undertone of the rosy glow of sunrise; warm PM colors have an undertone of the gold of sunset; and the Midday Colortime dips into both palettes, but never with a heavy hand.

For greatest harmony, colors blend best if they are in the same Colortime palette. For example: Shocking Pink has a definite blue undertone (AM). Apricot Cream is a light warm yellow-orange (PM). Unless you are going for a funky or deliberately discordant look, Shocking Pink and Apricot would not be a particularly pleasing combination because they are not in complete harmony. Living Coral and Apricot Cream are more effective together, because they have the same yellow-gold undertones. They are both PM colors.

Cool AM colors are often "sharper" than PM colors. Imagine the electric blue-green of a tropical ocean in the morning. These are AM colors. Now picture the deeper blue of the ocean at dusk, and you see PM colors. Next imagine that ocean at high noon. It is still a beautiful blue-green, but because of the sun's intensity, it appears a bit muted.

Undertones denote an underlying color within any given hue. Another word for undertone is cast, as in brown with a red cast.

Another example of pleasing combinations from the same Colortime palette is that of AM Violet Tulle with Prism Pink. If you want to choose a third color to harmonize, and you want to use a neutral tone, Frost Gray would be the most effective because of its cooling undertone.

Caramel and Cognac are handsome PM colors. A blending neutral would be Winter Wheat. A Midday combination of Grape Nectar, Mauve Mist, and Cloud Gray would be striking, yet subtle.

Purple, which blends red and blue, is a complex color. Redder, warmer purples blend best with the Sunset Colortime. Cooler, bluer purples blend best with Sunrise. Lighter and deeper tones blend best with the Sunlight Colortime. It can be difficult to see how much red or blue undertone is in a particular purple. If you're having "purple" trouble, look at your Colortime palette (which you can remove from this book, fold, and take with you when you shop). If you've forgotten it, your eye will have to be your guide. If the color you want to combine with a certain purple pleases your eye, go with it. Another trick for shopping when you don't have your color samples with you is to compare similar colors. If you hold one purple against another (or compare any two similar colors), the undertone will pop right out at you. It's always safest, of course, to keep your palette with you when you shop.

If you love a color that doesn't appear in your favorite Colortime, try it in a light-reflective fabric. The color will change according to the way the light bounces off it or is absorbed by it, creating "hills and valleys" of variation. It will be more flattering than the same color would be in a dull, matte finish.

Warm AM Colors: **Warm PM Colors:**

A pleasing warm AM combination of Violet Tulle, Prism Pink, and Lilac Marble alongsidea handsome warm PM combination of Cognac, Caramel, and Winter Wheat.

MIXING PALETTES

As a general rule, colors from the same palette blend best when used together. However, as with any rule, there is always the exception. The opposing Sunrise and Sunset palettes may be used together for deliberate discord or as attention-getters. This is a common technique used in areas other than fashion, such as advertising, packaging, signage, billboards, and websites.

Sometimes you will see Colortime palettes combined in costuming for stage, film, and television. The reason for this is to make the outfit unique so that long after you have forgotten how dramatic (or weird) the combinations were, you'll remember that show.

If the effect is blaring, like the psychedelics of the '60s, it is called "discordant." There was a time when AM brilliant green used with a PM hot purple was a popular combination. If the effect is not hard on the eyes, it is called a "hybrid" combination. Cool AM purples and warm PM spice tones are examples of hybrids that many designers have combined well, especially in intricate paisley prints.

Many combinations in the Sunlight Colortime are examples of interesting but subtle hybrid blends. The Sunlight palette shares peachy tones with the Sunset palette and cool lilac with the Sunrise palette. When used together, this unique combination is very flattering to the mixtures found in the Sunlight Colortime. They quietly claim your attention, but the more discordant mixtures of the Sunrise and Sunset palettes command it.

If you have an especially strong affinity for a particular Colortime, you might be perfectly content never to leave it. And you may choose not to. But if you have an especially favorite color, and it's not in your preferred Colortime palette, I would be the last person to advise you never to use it—never is a long, long time. It might evoke some wonderful childhood memory. If you always chose lemon gumdrops over every other flavor, you will remember the color as well as the taste. Lemon yellow brings back memories of delicious trips to the neighborhood candy store or Saturday afternoons at the movies with your best friend. If a lemony yellow is not a part of your Colortime palette, then scatter a bit of that color through your accessories. A pair of lemon-colored sandals or scarf can revive your happy memories every time you put them on.

The diagram below shows how Bright Rose from the AM Palette can be paired sparingly with a PM Fern.

The key to mixing Colortime palettes successfully is to keep one palette dominant and the other subordinate. The dominant Colortime palette should be 75 percent (or more) of the combination, and the subordinate Colortime should be 25 percent (or less). You may vary this somewhat. Try 85 percent or 90 percent dominant. You'll find these proportions also work well for any combination involving two colors, even if they come from the same Colortime.

Just as with music, discord is not always unpleasant, but our ears may tire of too much discordant sound. The same principle applies to color. You may deliberately combine Colortime palettes, but don't forget to do your math. Your eyes will tire of too much vibrant discord. And if your eyes get tired, you get tired, grumpy, and unsettled and start looking for a change.

If you want to experiment with a wild and crazy combination that equally combines two opposing palettes, buy a fun canvas bag or a summer shirt. If you get tired of it, you haven't invested a fortune. But if you have gone to the expense of putting together an entire outfit in those colors, you'll probably keep it tucked away in your closet. Choose combinations that you can live with for a long time. Most of us simply can't afford the time, energy, or money to keep changing.

EXPLODING OLD MYTHS—WHITE DOESN'T GO WITH EVERYTHING

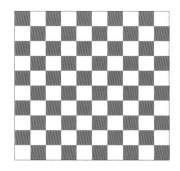

The diagram above shows how the white space between the bright orange squares appears to "shift" color.

Pure white is not a neutral color. It is dazzling and brilliant and impossible to ignore. It does not "go with everything." Because it is so highly reflective, especially in a fabric with a sheen, pristine white acts as a mirror as it reflects the color used immediately next to it. For example, if you use orange checks on a white background, the white warms up slightly, because the orange is so warm. Bright colors appear slightly duller next to pure white.

Mixing whites never works. Off-whites look dull and dingy next to pure white. Your beautiful antique lace blouse will look yellowed and faded next to a snow-white skirt, as will off-white gabardine pants next to a crisp white cotton shirt.

The AM Colortime palette can use pure whites better than the PM or Midday can, as it is a better blend with very cool light skin or as a crisp contrast to darker skin tones. For Middays, a bit of any pastel or neutral, depending on the other colors in the outfit, makes a good undertone to white, rendering it an off-white. And PM people find the creamier "winter whites" the best choice.

Pure white enlarges any area in which it is used, so when decorating your body or your bed, remember that anything amply upholstered will look larger in white! In clothing, a white sheer or semisheer fabric becomes an off-white. The undertone of the skin comes through and mutes the whiteness somewhat, making it a better choice for Midday or PM skin tones

The glare from a white shirt or blouse can make the face look pale. Women can compensate for this by wearing more makeup, unless they have very pink, very dark, or very olive skin, which provides good contrast to white in the AM palette. If you have very fair skin and you are a Sunrise, especially if you have light ash blonde hair, wearing a bit more blush can help to keep you from looking all of one color. If you love pure white, and you have a Midday or PM skin tone, save it for summer when your skin is tan, or if you are concerned about sun exposure, use a bronzer. Many people say they prefer white in summer, when tanned skin contrasts with the white and makes it more becoming. If you're a Midday or PM with dark skin, you can wear pure white year-round, but cream or pearly whites blend best with the other shades of your palette.

Pure white is also at its best at night, with its softening shadows. For Midday and PM men, Crossover Sky Blue, Sunlight, Bleached Sand, and Light Taupe are usually more flattering than pure white shirts. The AM skin may also wear those tints, since they are Crossovers.

Regardless of fashion's whims, pure white stockings look too stark. A subtle Sand is better. As for men—save your white socks for sneakers. White socks look nerdy with most other shoes.

Many performers love to wear dazzling white on stage because it is so luminous and attention-getting and the lighting seems to bounce right off it. But if you have PM coloring, dramatize your makeup and add color to your face so you won't look pale or sallow when you wear white.

YOU'LL LEARN MORE ABOUT HAIR AND MAKEUP COLOR IN THE NEXT CHAPTER.

3

WEARING YOUR COLORS: WHAT GOES WITH WHAT?

One of the greatest challenges is to combine colors effectively and attractively. Choosing a single color is much easier than deciding what goes with what.

Most of the old color rules have disappeared. Using blues with greens was once considered in terrible taste, and combining red with pink was a no-no. The only rule today is, "Never say never." Think in terms of guidelines rather than rules, which can hamper your creativity and take the fun out of being open to new ideas. Guidelines can give you the confidence to know how—and what—to combine.

WHAT GOES WITH WHAT?

The simplest and safest way to combine colors is to stick with those in the Colortime you have chosen, but here are some guidelines that professional designers use. Mastering them can help you create terrific combinations.

All color formulas are based on the color wheel. The Color Clock is designed to help you make happy marriages between harmonious and compatible colors. Of the many guidelines for color coordination, the least complicated and easiest to understand follow.

HARMONIOUS RELATIONS—ANALAGOUS COLORS

All colors are derived from the primary hues of red, yellow, and blue. If you mix equal parts of two of these primaries, you get the secondary colors of orange, green, and purple. They are color kin. Orange is the child of yellow and red, and purple results from the union of red and blue. Each of the secondary colors has a harmonious relationship with its "parent" colors.

The color wheel shows you the colors that are most closely related; these provide some of the easiest color schemes to work with. They are also the least apt to offend. These schemes are based on adjacent colors—for example, in the Sunset palette, yellow, yellow-orange, orange, and orange-red, which share the same undertone.

If you use green, yellow, and blue together (or orange, yellow, and red or purple, red, and blue), you have what is called a related or analagous color scheme.

If you want to expand your color "family" and stretch a bit further, you can add a cousin from either the yellow-green side, such as Fern for an interesting accent, or, from the red side, the touch of a warm red.

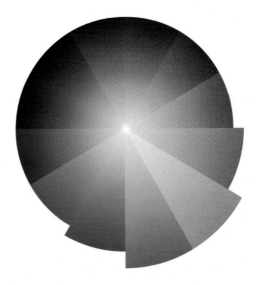

A Sunlight expanded analogous combination of Custard, Bisque, Peaches N' Cream, Simply Taupe, and a surprising Winter Pear.

Another example of an expanded analogous combination—this one from the cooler tones of the Sunrise family—is neighboring shades of blue, blue-purple, purple, and fuchsia. An accent of a shocking pink lives up to its name, while a clear, cool blue acts as a chill factor. An analogous example from the Sunlight family is a custard yellow, velvety bisque, and creamy peach, with the added depth of a deep taupe and the surprising bite of a pear-skin green.

If you're thinking: "How am I going to remember all of this?" don't worry. The prints and patterns where you are most likely to see analogous combinations often come ready made, and chances are you'll gravitate naturally to those that belong to your Colortime.

THANK YOU FOR THE COMPLEMENT

• **Com-ple-ment:** that which completes or makes perfect.

Complementary or contrasting colors are those situated directly across from each other on the standard color wheel. They are called complements because they complete each other. Green, for example, is the complement to red and never looks greener than when it is next to red. Conversely, red appears reddest when next to green. A red rose in a print seems even redder when set against a green leafy backdrop.

The color wheel illustrates the complementary colors. Orange complements blue, and yellow complements purple. When used in the brightest intensities, complementary colors provide instant "zing" and can be real showstoppers. The complementary color effect is a major reason for advising redheads to wear green.

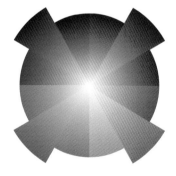

COM-PLE-MENT:
THAT WHICH COMPLETES

Complementary combinations can be superdramatic, but they can also be strident in their demand for attention. People with outgoing personalities often love them. When graphic artists design packaging, they use the brightest intensities of complementary colors when they want to command attention. On your next trip to the market, look at the brilliant array of detergent boxes all begging for your attention. Notice how many are done in the sharpest complementary combinations.

Complementaries can be used to wonderful advantage, but they can boomerang as well. If your skin flushes easily and you have a ruddy complexion, bright green next to your face will bring out the pink (light red) in your skin. The green should be lightened or deepened for a more flattering effect. When the intensity of one or both of the complementaries is muted, the combination is much easier on the eyes. For example, the AM Bright Rose and Emerald combination is less jarring optically than the same rose when paired with Electric Green. Deepening a vivid Sunset orange and combining it with a deep greenish-blue is very effective as you can soften the shock of complementaries by choosing unexpected tints and shades of the two opposing colors.

If you do combine palettes, remember our dominance and subordination guideline: whether combining colors from opposite Colortimes or within the same one, one color is always the star and takes center stage, while the other is the supporting player.

When intense or strongly contrasting colors are offset by neutral colors, the combination becomes much richer. The neutrals enhance the brighter colors by making them easier to view. For example: AM Vivid Viola and Daiquiri Green might be great fun in a Hawaiian print shirt, but when these hues are mixed with gray, taupe, or beige, the combination becomes more intriguing and gains a quiet neutral shade to use as an accessory color. Sunlight palettes have no really "vibrating" contrasts, but that doesn't mean there is no drama in this Colortime. Think Cornflower Blue and Cornsilk. And if you're dressing for a holiday party at Christmas, think Verdant Green velvet enhanced by sparkling Baroque Rose crystal drop earrings.
If you use complementary combinations within your Colortime, you won't tire of these colors quickly. However, if strong impact and high octane are what you're looking for (as in adrenalin-pumping snow or surf ware), combining opposite Colortimes of Sunrise and Sunset will definitely ratchet up the voltage.

Sunrise complements of Vivid Viola and Daiquiri Green softened with a Neutral Gray.

PHOTO: GREG BOYD

Green will keep redheads from fading away into beige; but since most "red" hair is closer to orange, bright blues and blue-greens are actually more complementary,

What to Do If You Are Fading Away

As you follow the circle of the color wheel, think of your own coloring. Complementary colors in your Colortime can help to keep you from fading away (as we all do to some extent after a long winter with little sun or a bout with the flu). Blue eyes are enhanced by browns, warm pinks, oranges, and corals. Green eyes are flattered by wines, pinks, and reds. Hazel eyes are chameleons that pick up and reflect many of the colors that are worn near them. They often combine many colors, but one color usually predominates. Complementary colors are very effective with hazel eyes and can virtually change their color.

Brown eyes and hair are complemented by greens, especially blue-greens. Since gray is a neutral, it really doesn't have a complementary color as such, but it is enhanced by touches of color. Nor does black have a true complement, but both bright hues and white contrast effectively with it.

If you are blonde, purpled shades and tints will make you look blonder.

ONE COLOR—MONOCHROMATICS

A monochromatic color scheme uses only one hue in varying shades and tints. The secret of a successful monochromatic scheme is to select all of the variations of this single hue from the same Colortime to avoid clashing undertones.

If you are working with varying shades of AM blue-red, for example, colors such as Almond Blossom and Cerise look best together because they have the same blue undertone. A good PM orangey combination is Ginger with Living Coral. An attractive Midday combination is Mauve Mist and Purple Haze.

Weddings are excellent occasions for being creative with monochromatic color schemes. The mother of the bride can be lovely in varying tones of an AM Cyclamen with undertones from the same Colortime. When coordinating wedding parties, wearing monochromatic colors from the same Colortime can be very effective. It's much easier to choose flowers, the wedding pictures are lovely because everyone's colors blend so well, and a beautiful occasion becomes even more beautiful.

In monochromatic color schemes, light and bright shades and tints draw the eye first. So unless you want your feet to be the focal point, use darker colors at the lower part of your body and lighter and brighter shades as you move toward your face, which then becomes the focal point.

In the case of the bride's mother, who plans to wear Cyclamen silk with an overlay of see-through chiffon, the violet-pink tones of the top of the dress gradually deepen toward the hem. Her shoes are a slightly deeper shade than the hem. If she chose to wear a sparkling hair ornament or chandelier earrings, they should be as light as, or lighter than, the top of her dress. Darkening the colors at the lower part of the body gives stability to the figure, makes it appear slimmer, and directs attention to the face.

The ultimate monochromatic color scheme uses only one color with very little variation. The effect can be quite stark or even severe, but it is very dramatic. Using a variety of textures and shapes can help to avoid too much sameness. For example, picture someone with warm, deep brown hair in the Sunset palette. She has warm amber eyes and creamy skin and is wearing smooth brown wool flannel pants, a matching loopy soft angora sweater, deep brown suede shoes, a supple brown leather jacket, and gold jewelry. It's all very simple and chic in beautiful chocolate tones, but it's hardly boring because of the variety of textures and finishes.

A Sunrise monochromatic combination of Sachet Pink, Bright Rose, and Almond Blossom.

Neutral Territory

Neutral colors can make very effective monochromatic combinations, but they can also be tricky. It's usually not too difficult to find tan pants, a camel corduroy jacket, and a beige sweater with the same undertones. It is well worth the effort. Your Colortime palette can help you avoid expensive mistakes in undertone.

Have you ever bought a shirt in a neutral shade to go with slacks of the same color, only to get home and find that they don't go together at all? Although it isn't necessary to find colors that match perfectly (it's better to look for a blend rather than a match because dye lots are never exactly the same), undertones should always blend.

Gray is another great neutral that lends itself well to monochromatic combinations. There are warm PM grays and cool AM grays, but the most versatile grays of all are the balanced, crossover Neutral Gray and Charcoal Gray. These are the grays that blend with every Colortime. (See examples in Crossover Colors, chapter 2.)

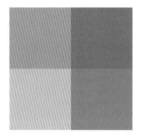

Shades of taupe—the budget stretcher. Clockwise: Warm Taupe, Taupe Gray, Simply Taupe and Light Taupe

Terrific Taupe

Taupe is the neutral that gets the gold star for versatility. It is the happy union of beige and gray, with several different undertones. Some taupes lean a bit toward gray, while others are slightly warmer.

Because of their versatility, however, and the fact that they are actually a blend of two neutrals, most taupes are Crossover Colors. The French call it "greige." Once you discover taupe (if you haven't yet), you'll wonder how you ever managed without it. Taupe shades may also be called Mushroom or Chanterelle or they may include another descriptive word, such as Plaza Taupe or Simply Taupe.

Neutral colors are excellent budget stretchers because they blend well, are basic and dependable, aren't trendy, are never offensive, and make excellent background colors. They are also marvelous foils for bright accents. It's much easier on the bank account to use temporarily tempting colors in accents like scarves, sandals, jewelry, and hair accessories, which cost relatively little and can be changed much more easily than can large pieces.

MONOCHROMATIC LOOKS CAN BE STRIKING AS ILLUSTRATED BY THIS RICH COLLECTION OF VARYING BROWN TONES

TWO COLORS—DUOCHROMATICS

A duochromatic combination consists of just two colors. There are also two basic guidelines to remember here. The first is that the eye is drawn to the area where the two colors meet. A dark bathing suit may make your figure appear smaller, but it will also draw attention to the upper thigh, where the light color of the skin meets the dark of the suit, or vice versa. If you are chunkier than you'd like to be, a bathing suit that matches your skin tone is more flattering because it blends with your body and presents no line of demarcation to draw the eye.

The second guideline again focuses on the basic math of one dominant and one subordinate color—75 percent or slightly more of one shade and 25 percent or less of another.

These proportions are more pleasing, because they set up a dominant color theme. For example, a navy interview suit with red shoes, red bag, red blouse, and red jewelry would be much too busy and too much "overkill." The eye is drawn to too many areas at once, and you don't know where to look first. A potential employer, especially in a more "serious" industry, might find all that red too theatrical. He or she doesn't want to hire a drama queen. Your colors speak volumes.

A better choice is to make the suit, since it already covers so much area, the dominant color. The accessories should be navy. The blouse could stay red, but a more interesting and coordinated option is a patterned combination of navy and red. Or, instead of a suit, try a navy skirt and a patterned jacket.

Another example of good color proportions is introducing accessories into a too simple, unadorned look. A wine-colored, hip-length sweater and gray pants divides the body in half. Without any accessories or a change in texture, it's pretty boring. Silver chains, hoop earrings, and some silver bracelets and rings establish the dominance of gray (and its "sister," silver) and really pulls the outfit together.

The effectiveness of duochromatics can be in the simplicity of combining just two colors. Just as with monochromatics, one or both of the colors may vary in value or intensity.

Complementary combinations can also be considered duochromatic, but they are only those that oppose each other on the color wheel.

When you add a touch of rosy pink (a lighter variation of wine) to this wine and gray duo, it's still a duochromatic combination, but now it offers more variety.

A duochromatic combination may be very dramatic in its simplicity. A traditional example is black and white. Jet Black is a Crossover color. If you're a stickler for precision, blue-black is specifically AM, umber or warmer blacks are PM, and Midday is a combination of both. But it is really difficult, especially in poor lighting, to differentiate between them. Chances are that if you can't tell what the undertone is, no one else can either.

Finding similar undertones in black only becomes important when you are combining blacks in the same outfit. We've all had the experience of putting a black sweater with black pants only to discover that the blacks didn't work together. They were from different Colortimes.

The best combinations of black and white are black and pure white for AM; black and cream white for PM; and black and ivory for Midday. The most dramatic use of black and white I have ever seen was at a party given after the premiere of a film at a major film studio. (The picture was terrible, but the *party* was terrific.)

The tables were done in black tablecloths with white place settings and white tapered candles. White camellias, gardenias, mums, tulips, and roses, in single-faceted crystal bud vases of various heights, were placed on gleaming mirrors in the center of each table. Everything sparkled and glimmered; it was truly breathtaking.

Each of the guests was asked to wear black or white. The men wore black tuxes with gleaming white shirts, and the women wore long black or white gowns.

Simple, unadorned, stark black can be fabulous in clothing whenever it provides strong contrast, such as on redheads, blondes, or silver—or white-haired—wearers in any Colortime. It is also wonderful on fair or rosy AM skin, light creamy PM skin, and the ivory skin of Midday. For the rest of us, black needs a touch of pizzazz near the face, such as a hint of red in a patterned tie or the contrast of a light or brightly colored shirt, or the sparkle of faceted jewelry around the neck.

By placing the third color in the scarf or tie, you draw attention to the face. If you add this accent in a belt, the waist becomes the focal point. Use the accent color wherever it is the most flattering.

THREE COLORS—TRICHROMATICS

A trichromatic color scheme uses three colors. One color dominates (approximately 75 percent), the second is subordinate (15 percent), and just a touch is used as the third (10 percent). This third color can be used effectively to draw the eye to a given area, making it a focal point. If you were cooking, you'd call it a "pinch."

If your legs aren't as shapely as you'd like them to be, or your feet are bigger than you'd like them to be, don't wear an accent color in your shoes, particularly in bright tones and, most particularly, in white. White is perceived as a brilliant and enlarging color. Dazzling white is okay on a tennis court, but white needs to connect with a predominantly white outfit or white pants. With other AM colors, pure white can look crisp and clean in the summer or in the tropics, but, as I have pointed out, white is not a neutral and doesn't go with everything. So ignore that old, "It's summer and I must have white shoes to go with everything," routine. If you're not using AM colors, you don't need white at all. Taupe is really smarter for all Colortime palettes—even when worn with white. You especially don't want white shoes to blink on and off under a darker outfit.

One particular three-color combination is called "triadic." This plan uses three equidistant colors on the standard color wheel. A conventional triadic scheme of Crossover Navy Blue, True Red, and a sliver of Sunlight might appear in a pattern. These are all Crossover Colors that have wide appeal for all Colortimes, especially to men. Think of the guys in comedy sitcoms who favor those comfortable plaids in triadic combos. A less traditional (and more interesting Crossover combo) is Pale Khaki, Beaujolais, and Navy Blue.

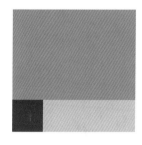

A Crossover trichromatic combination of Faded Denim, True Red, and Pale Khaki.

DRAW ATTENTION TO YOUR FACE WITH A SCARF OR TIE IN ONE OF YOUR COLORTIME COLORS

MULTICOLORS—POLYCHROMATICS

When a combination includes more than three colors, it is referred to as polychromatic. The combining of more than three solid hues can seem very "spotty" and is often distracting to the eye, yet groups of colors can be combined effectively in clothing. Prints, plaids, and tweeds often successfully mix many more than three colors

Polychromatic schemes are most harmonious when one hue, such as the background color, is predominant. For example, a multifloral printed linen skirt in the southwestern desert PM shades of Terra Cotta (background), Apricot Cream, Honey Gold, Muted Clay, and a touch of Deep Peacock Blue can be used with a Terra Cotta blouse. Terra Cotta suede shoes as accessories and earrings in turquoise-cast Deep Peacock Blue complete the scheme. Terra Cotta becomes the predominant color because it occupies the largest area.

In clothing, a typical polychromatic combination for men or women is wool tweed with a Crossover Neutral Gray background interspersed with tiny random flecks of Navy Blue, Beaujolais, and Pineneedle. Any of these colors will work in a coordinating blouse or shirt.

INSTANT IRRITANTS AND DRAMATIC DISCORD

For color at its most harmonious, avoid using opposite Colortime palettes of AM and PM *in equal amounts* in their brightest intensities; they will fight for attention on your body. However, discord can be very dramatic if used in the right proportions. For example, a paisley design of a dominant and deliciously warm Sunset Cognac can have a splash of Sunrise's vibrant blue-greens to create some exotic excitement, and a sprinkle of Ginger from the Sunset palette against a dominant Sunrise Prism Violet is certainly different and, very often, theatrical. Discord can work if you follow the guidelines of dominance and subordination. But it's not for the faint-hearted or basically practical person. It takes an adventurous person, with a love of the offbeat or "quirky," to use odd or highly unusual combinations, but you can also create unusual combinations within your Colortime and not run the risk of looking eccentric.

What if somebody gives you a gift that is a discordant combination of colors? You may not particularly like it, but if your brand-new significant other's mother gives it to you, you feel you have to show up in it. Let's assume that it's a bulky (and itchy) wool V-neck cardigan in her (not your) favorite shade of mossy green. You are a Midday and really are not turned on at all to that particular green. You feel it makes you look and feel kind of nauseous What can you do?

If you wear a patterned shirt with the collar showing in the V-neck, it will not only solve the itchies, it will also accomplish what I call "breaking the color line." Allowing other colors next to your face to reflect in your hair, skin, and eyes keeps the yellow-green from being right up under your chin. The shirt might have a single line of yellow-green running through the plaid; the other colors can be softened Midday colors such as Dusty Lavender, Powder Pink, and Whisper White. The small amount of yellow-green in the shirt blends with the sweater. Remember, it doesn't have to match perfectly. The other colors are all in your Colortime, so you have a happy solution.

THE MOST BASIC BASICS

To stretch your budget, use neutrals, basics and Crossover Colors. Make them a vital part of your combinations, as most are classics and work really well as accessories.

One color should be dominant, the second subordinate, and the third an accent. Any color in your palette's combinations may be the dominant, subordinate or accent color. See chapters 2, 3 and 4 for coordinating more than three colors, plus additional "how-to's" on putting attractive combinations into your wardrobe.

Okay, Okay … we know it sounds boring, but if you really want to reorganize and simplify, basics are at least a place to start. This works for business, travel, and, yes, even for casual clothes. Basics are always a beginning.

Start with a two-color (duochromatic) plan. Crossover Colors are always the dependable backbone for your first color choice. To keep it even simpler, the second color choice can also come from the Crossovers. For example, Jet Black skirt, shoes, belt, bag, and pantyhose with a Teal turtleneck. You have the option of either a Jet Black jacket or a sweater. Another option is a Crossover Teal jacket or a twin sweater that matches the Teal turtleneck. Jet Black is obviously the most practical choice as you can wear it with so many other options as well, but Teal might be the choice for a second purchase.

If you add a third color (trichromatic), you can also dip into the Crossovers. Maybe in addition to your Teal sweater (or sweaters), you add a striped blouse of Jet Black, Teal, and Light Taupe. The blouse can be worn with the skirt or over the turtleneck and opens other possibilities of combinations. Your next purchase can be Light Taupe pants and jacket, bought together so they are from the same "dye lot" (as they say in the textile industry), and you're on your way.

You are certainly not limited to staying within the Crossovers, but it does help to simplify your life. And the basic colors are not limited to just the office or for business travel. Think about a group of basics for a holiday in Hawaii. You certainly want to get fun colors into that mix, but starting with sandy-colored shorts, sandals, and a big tote bag leads to all sorts of possibilities for coordinating colors from your Colortime palette. The secondary color, like True Red, Sunlight, or Navy Blue can come from the Crossovers as well, but you might opt to dip into your Colortime palettes.

Your first choice of a basic color depends on the climate where you live and the season of the year, although regional and seasonal color choices have really "blurred." So go for a marriage of the comfort level, appropriateness, and the most flattering colors that work for you. And when adding new colors into the mix, definitely go for colors in your personal Colortime.

GOOF-PROOF COMBINATIONS

Choosing color is rarely about one simple choice but more often a combination of colors. And that's where the challenge comes in. If you absolutely love color and have a real talent for creating combinations, this is always the fun part. But if you're not too adventurous and find the whole effort really exhausting and/or confusing, you just need a jump-start to your efforts. And that's where the "Goof-Proof" combinations come in.

Use the Goof-Proof combinations that follow as a guideline to get your creative juices going. Even if you have a great eye for color, some of the combinations might give you some more colorful options. As you will discover later in the book, your personality definitely enters into your choices, so some of the combinations will feel just right, and others won't feel as comfortable. But keep an open mind and use this guide to play with the possibilities.

Proportions are important. One color is dominant, the second color is subordinate, and the third color is an accent or touch. There may be more than three colors, but this is generally within a print, a pattern, or stripes so that the entire outfit doesn't get too "spotty."

Play with color combinations, just as a child does with a box of crayons. You might come up with combinations that are not listed. You can open yourself up to a whole new creative experience. Don't be concerned about how someone else might do it. Choose your Colortime and let your colors be an expression of you. Keep an open mind to the excitement of new and interesting color combinations in your chosen Colortime and see how you can come more alive with color!

To my male readers:

It might be difficult for you to relate to colors with "feminine" names like Shocking Pink or Violet Tulle. Just think of those vivid preppie cotton knit or dress shirts in cotton candy colors and you'll get the picture. Forget the names—just use your palette as your guide. After all, women have been using so-called masculine colors like Charcoal Gray and Navy Blue for years, and it hasn't made them any less ladylike!

SUNRISE (AM) GOOF PROOF COMBINATIONS

The twenty-four combinations illustrated below are among the best "goof-proof" possibilities in the Sunrise palette. Some are classic and conservative, appropriate for a business suit, like Navy Blue, Bright White and Cerise. Others are more fun and creative, great in a bathing suit, like Blue Atoll, Capri Breeze and Daiquiri Green. Choose the combinations that suit your needs, but use the following combinations to open yourself to new possibilities. For example, one of the best ways to recycle a favorite Navy Blue jacket is to wear it with Electric Green and Blue Jewel. It will seem new and fresh again.

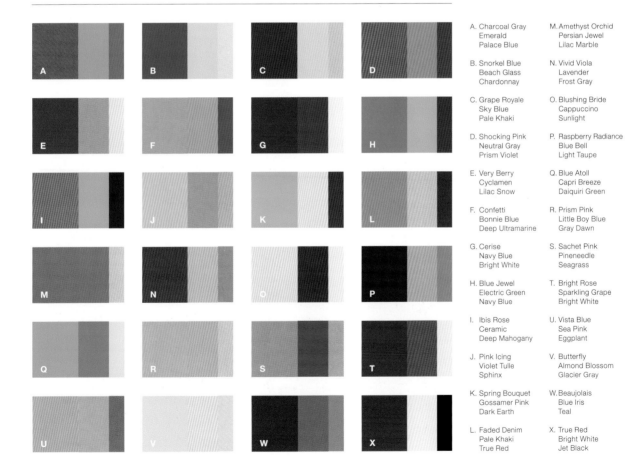

A. Charcoal Gray
   Emerald
   Palace Blue

B. Snorkel Blue
   Beach Glass
   Chardonnay

C. Grape Royale
   Sky Blue
   Pale Khaki

D. Shocking Pink
   Neutral Gray
   Prism Violet

E. Very Berry
   Cyclamen
   Lilac Snow

F. Confetti
   Bonnie Blue
   Deep Ultramarine

G. Cerise
   Navy Blue
   Bright White

H. Blue Jewel
   Electric Green
   Navy Blue

I. Ibis Rose
   Ceramic
   Deep Mahogany

J. Pink Icing
   Violet Tulle
   Sphinx

K. Spring Bouquet
   Gossamer Pink
   Dark Earth

L. Faded Denim
   Pale Khaki
   True Red

M. Amethyst Orchid
   Persian Jewel
   Lilac Marble

N. Vivid Viola
   Lavender
   Frost Gray

O. Blushing Bride
   Cappuccino
   Sunlight

P. Raspberry Radiance
   Blue Bell
   Light Taupe

Q. Blue Atoll
   Capri Breeze
   Daiquiri Green

R. Prism Pink
   Little Boy Blue
   Gray Dawn

S. Sachet Pink
   Pineneedle
   Seagrass

T. Bright Rose
   Sparkling Grape
   Bright White

U. Vista Blue
   Sea Pink
   Eggplant

V. Butterfly
   Almond Blossom
   Glacier Gray

W. Beaujolais
   Blue Iris
   Teal

X. True Red
   Bright White
   Jet Black

SUNSET (PM) GOOF PROOF COMBINATIONS

The twenty-four combinations illustrated here are among the best "goof-proof" possibilities in the Sunset palette. Some are classic and conservative—best in a business suit, like Winter Wheat, Camel and Black. Others are better suited for athletics or outdoor play, like Cappuccino, Cadmium Orange, and Iris Orchid. Choose whatever seems to suit the occasion, but try to use these suggestions to open you up to all the possibilities of your palette. For example, the best way to update taupe pants is to wear them in unexpected combinations, like Warm Taupe, Bougainvillea and Sunkist Coral.

A. Cranberry
   Green Moss
   Pampas

B. Peach
   Ginger
   Hot Chocolate

C. Tigerlily
   Moroccan Blue
   Cappuccino

D. Light Taupe
   Muted Clay
   Fern

E. Earth Red
   Caramel
   Teal

F. Amber Yellow
   Living Coral
   Doe

G. Pineneedle
   Feldspar
   Pale Khaki

H. Doe
   Sky Blue
   Winter White

I. Burnt Coral
   Moonlite Mauve
   Cognac

J. Sunkist Coral
   Bougainvillea
   Warm Taupe

K. Fiesta
   Sepia
   Mimosa

L. True Red
   Bleached Sand
   Jet Black

M. Della Robbia Blue
   Fern
   Sepia

N. Byzantium
   Honey Gold
   Coriander

O. Bellini
   Seagrass
   Faded Denim

P. Cayenne
   Magenta Haze
   Dark Earth

Q. Deep Periwinkle
   Camel
   Latté

R. Pesto
   Celestial
   Eggplant

S. Apricot Cream
   Chateau Gray
   Charcoal Gray

T. Beaujolais
   Sauterne
   Moonlight Blue

U. Iris Orchid
   Cadmium Orange
   Cappuccino

V. Deep Peacock Blue
   Bright Cartreuse
   Navy Blue

W. Terra Cotta
   Fir
   Taupe Gray

X. Camel
   Jet Black
   Winter Wheat

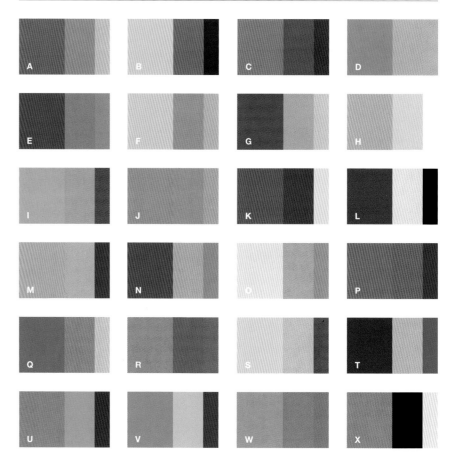

SUNLIGHT (MIDDAY) GOOF PROOF COMBINATIONS

The twenty-four combinations illustrated here are among the best "goof-proof" possibilities in the Sunlight palette. Some are classic and conservative—appropriate for business—such as Deep Taupe, Simply Taupe and Desert Rose. Others are unique—great for prints, like Winter Pear, Silver Lake Blue, and Red Violet. Choose whatever fits the mood or the occasion, but try to use these suggested combinations to open yourself up to all the possibilities of your palette. For example, perk up a pair of tired (but still so comfortable) Pale Khaki fleece pants by wearing them with Jadeite and Bisque.

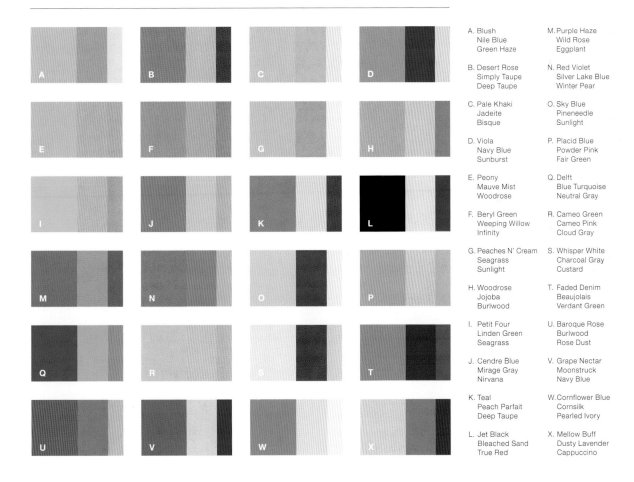

A. Blush
   Nile Blue
   Green Haze

B. Desert Rose
   Simply Taupe
   Deep Taupe

C. Pale Khaki
   Jadeite
   Bisque

D. Viola
   Navy Blue
   Sunburst

E. Peony
   Mauve Mist
   Woodrose

F. Beryl Green
   Weeping Willow
   Infinity

G. Peaches N' Cream
   Seagrass
   Sunlight

H. Woodrose
   Jojoba
   Burlwood

I. Petit Four
   Linden Green
   Seagrass

J. Cendre Blue
   Mirage Gray
   Nirvana

K. Teal
   Peach Parfait
   Deep Taupe

L. Jet Black
   Bleached Sand
   True Red

M. Purple Haze
   Wild Rose
   Eggplant

N. Red Violet
   Silver Lake Blue
   Winter Pear

O. Sky Blue
   Pineneedle
   Sunlight

P. Placid Blue
   Powder Pink
   Fair Green

Q. Delft
   Blue Turquoise
   Neutral Gray

R. Cameo Green
   Cameo Pink
   Cloud Gray

S. Whisper White
   Charcoal Gray
   Custard

T. Faded Denim
   Beaujolais
   Verdant Green

U. Baroque Rose
   Burlwood
   Rose Dust

V. Grape Nectar
   Moonstruck
   Navy Blue

W. Cornflower Blue
   Cornsilk
   Pearled Ivory

X. Mellow Buff
   Dusty Lavender
   Cappuccino

4

HOW TO GET THE LOOK:
PERSONAL SIGNATURE COLORS
ACCESSORIZING WITH COLOR
CLOTHES TO GO

When you discover how to add your personal colors to those all-important wardrobe components—your "Signature Colors" and accessories (shoes, stockings, handbags, belts, and jewelry)—your personal style will be set! Let's start with what I call "Signature Colors."

Everyone has a personal color signature that is created by wearing colors that repeat or enhance your hair, skin, and eye color. By assembling these special shades in your clothes and accessories, you'll create a core of colors that has your personal stamp (or style).

For example, if you are a Sunlight and your hair is medium brown streaked with blonde tones and you have changeable chameleon-like eyes that range from blue to green and a rosy skin tone, you can display your Signature Colors by wearing jeans and a tweed jacket that has flecks of brown and beige, a blue-green shirt, and a tie or scarf with those same colors and a touch of rose. These colors are truly you––a wonderful way to capitalize on your own coloring and make you stand out from the crowd. This doesn't mean that you wear exactly the same combination of colors all the time. That would soon seem stale. But it does mean that you have created a look that you can always depend on by varying the contrasts, patterns, and some of the colors themselves.

Trendy touches can always be added, such as substituting a yellow-green shirt for the blue-green, which will make your chameleon eyes look yellow-green. It's fun and a creative challenge to keep your look fresh and updated. It's using color as a vital and memorable part of your personal picture. Here are some additional tips for selecting Signature Colors based on specific natural coloring.

Sunrise

If you have hair, skin, and eyes with very little contrast, such as very dark skin, eyes, and hair that appear almost black, there are actually other undertones present. Extremely dark skin and hair may appear to be blue-black, for instance, so a Jet Black or Navy Blue sweater and pants accented with a Vista Blue shirt and a touch of Bright White to add sharp contrast (and enhance the white of the eyes) will look terrific.

If your skin is a deep dark brown, a brownish-black, such as Deep Mahogany, will look subtly striking. An Emerald green shirt will complement coffee-colored skin, and a touch of Bright White will add the most flattering contrast.

If you hair is silver, your eyes are a light blue, and your skin is fair, there is nothing like the drama of Jet Black, Navy Blue, Eggplant, or Charcoal

Gray worn with contrasting Bright White, Sky Blue, or Glacier Gray and a truly vibrant touch of a Bright Rose.

Asian AM skin tones are flattered by colors complementing the olive base in the skin. Reds and roses, such as Very Berry and Gossamer Pink, as well as vibrant tones, such as Raspberry Radiance, will reflect a healthy glow onto your skin. These shades will flatter dark hair and dark eyes as well.

Sunset

Redheads, by virtue of their unique coloring, can't help but attract attention. If you are a copper-toned redhead with cream-colored skin and amber eyes, you know that the very same shades are magical on you. They are definitely your Signature Colors, but you've already discovered that, haven't you?

If you are a honey blonde with creamy skin coloring and deep blue-green eyes, a classic combo for you is Apricot Cream, Deep Peacock Blue, and Honey Gold.

Sunlight

Sandy-haired people with beige skin tones and brown eyes invariably go for the neutrals, especially in beige and beige-taupes. Although they are a reflection of your own coloring, if you wear them consistently and with very little contrast, you will disappear into the woodwork. Wear these classic tones, but add a touch of contrast, something memorable, especially when you're on a job interview. Most likely you will lean to mid-tone, softer shades as they are most flattering to your coloring. An uncomplicated neutral such as Simply Taupe, for example, is wonderful with shades like Jadeite to complement eyes and hair and a dash of Dusty Lavender highlighting on the lips and cheeks.

YOUR SIGNATURE COLORS
WILL SET YOUR STYLE

ACCESSORIZING WITH COLOR

Shoes

Unless you're doing a really playful or casual look, a good "when in doubt" guideline is to keep shoe colors the same tone as your hemline or wear a deeper shade. At one time in fashion, that was the only way to go.

Now there are some exceptions to this rule:

1. When you wear pants, shoes are not as outstanding as they are with a skirt or a dress because you're creating an elongated line through the leg. But let your eye be the judge. If shoes are too bright, light, white, or shiny, they may be distracting and bring the eye to the feet first when you don't want your feet to be a focal point—especially if you're self-conscious about your shoe size.

2. When wearing over-the-calf (not short) boots, the leg appears elongated, so it is not necessary to match the hemline. However, the figure is lengthened even more when the hemline and boot do match. For an even longer line, match hosiery color to boots.

3. Boots can blend, match, or relate to something in the top of the outfit—for example, a Crossover print shirt of True Red, Faded Denim, and Seagrass with jeans and red boots.

4. When wearing a light- to medium-value or neutral color, neutral shoes work best. They may be somewhat lighter, darker, or the same tone as the hemline—for example, a PM coral dress with light camel shoes or an AM lilac dress with gray shoes. Taupe is definitely the most versatile of all neutrals, since it goes with almost all colors, except very dark shades.

5. Very dark hues in an outfit do need dark shoe colors. Black, navy, dark purples, reds, wines, greens, charcoal gray, brown, and other dark colors need to be supported by dark shoes. Neutral shoes are too light. In fashion parlance, this is called stability—balancing the darker shades on the upper body with those of the lower body. This is especially important to anyone who is wider below than she is above. Although black is a given, the deeper Crossover shades provide some interesting alternatives.

6. Shoes may be dyed to match, especially when the color is unusual. This is a very dramatic or fun approach, but it's not absolutely necessary. If you like to "play" with colors, experiment on an older pair of shoes in fairly good condition. Most shoe repair shops carry color dyes. If you're not too confident about your artistic abilities, let the shoemaker do it for you. A deep berry long dress might be beautiful with matching shoes (if you can get them to match!), but strappy black sandals work, too, and are far more practical.

7. Metallic finishes are also a good solution. Silver metallics look best with cool colors, and gold works best with warm colors. There are also some "pewterized" shades that seem to have a blend of both gold and silver. Because they seem to go with so many other colors, they make a great addition to your wardrobe. But they aren't easy to find.

Hosiery

A good rule of thumb is to blend the color of your panty hose with the color of your shoes. It makes you look "leggier," and it's especially sexy in neutrals such as taupe. Models and actresses often use this look on stage.

If you're the trendy type and want to use light panty hose when they're in style, use something light at the top of the body, such as a blouse, scarf, collar, or jewelry, as a connecting link to your face and to create good balance.

Dark panty hose do not always make your legs look slimmer, and light panty hose do not always make your legs look heavier. It depends on how you put the look together. Navy panty hose under a light gray skirt will draw the eye directly to the point where the two colors come together and enlarge the legs by creating a horizontal line, but sand panty hose under a sand skirt create a longer line, especially when coordinated with sand shoes.

BLEND THE COLOR OF
YOUR PANTY HOSE WITH
THE COLOR OF YOUR SHOES

We've all had the experience of buying panty hose, putting them on, looking in the mirror, and thinking, "Something is wrong here." Here are some helpful pointers about the basic "families" of panty hose colors.

If you are in doubt about your Colortime hosiery, compare several shades and you'll see the undertones. Be sure to take along your detachable Colortime palette.

Trends come and go, but these are still the classic combinations:

Taupe

This is the gray-beige, "when in doubt" shade that blends with so many clothing colors. It's at its best with taupe and light to mid-tones of gray, blue, or green. It's also a good shade when you'd rather not wear anything too dark with blacks and browns.

Beige to Medium Brown

These shades go best with bone, off-white, tan, etc. Be careful to choose the proper undertones. Generally, the Sunrises are cooler, Sunsets warmer, and Sunlights a combination of the two. Cool pinky Sunrise beige panty hose will not look good with a warm Sunset camel shoe; your legs will look red.

Gray to Off-Black

These shades go best with gray and black shoes and sometimes with navy. Avoid beige tones with gray or black.

Neutral

The best way to describe a neutral panty hose is to say that it matches your skin shade. From fair to dark, this is the panty hose to wear when you want your leg color to be as unobtrusive as possible. For example, a slinky red dress with matching shoes makes enough of a statement without adding red stockings, too. Neutral hosiery is also worn with white shoes. The darker your skin tone, the darker the "neutrals" will be. When you feel dark stockings are too heavy-looking for spring and summer for darker-toned shoes, neutrals are a good option.

Deep Reds, Purples, Blues, Greens, Browns

Outfits in these shades need panty hose that blend. But, again, in spring and summer, neutrals will work.

Very Dark and Very Light

Trend colors, such as pastels and dark or bright opaques, will change according to the latest fashion. The general guideline is to blend to your shoe color; but for a fun look, blend to a color in the top of your outfit.

Handbags

There was a time when handbags had to match shoes. Now the key word is "mood." As long as both the bag *and* shoes are sporty or dressy, forget all the old rules. The bag can still match your shoes, but it can also be lighter or somewhat darker, as long as the undertone is similar.

The neutral color is the most favored, practical way to go, especially in taupe. Your bag can also match something in the body of your outfit, such as a belt, or it can be in a pattern that blends with your shoes or outfit. If you have invested in a (real) designer signature bag, you might feel you want to get your money's worth from your investment by wearing it with everything. That's understandable, but sometimes the blend of colors just doesn't work. Sorry!

Belts

Belts can be an interesting color accent. They can match your shoes, your bag, or a color in the body of your outfit, or they can blend with other accessories like jewelry or scarves. A belt will draw attention to the waist if its color contrasts with the background. That same color should be repeated in one or two additional spots on your body. Remember, a solid accent color should be used in no more than three places on your body or the look becomes spotty and distracting.

Jewelry

Since there are warm and cool colors in all palettes, silver and gold have a place in each Colortime. The type of finish determines where it looks best. Shiny silvers and platinums work well with the cool AM jewel tones, and shiny gold with the warm AM tones. There are more warm colors in the PM, so Florentine golds and deep coppers complement the warm tones; and pewters and brushed and antique silver look best with cool PM colors. Middays can use either, but favor the delustered finishes.

There are some really wonderful "designer" looks in jewelry that combine gold and silver. They are the most versatile pieces of jewelry you can

Silver and gold can be worn together, but it's best to keep the finishes compatible, such as brassy gold with shiny silver or brushed gold with antiqued silver.

SILVER AND GOLD NECKLACE: DONNA LINE; PHOTO: STEVE GIRALT

own; but, again, proportion is the basic rule that makes combining metallic surfaces work. Silver is cool and gold is warm, so one should be dominant. For instance, the piece can be approximately 75 percent warm or 75 percent cool, with the opposite temperature making up about 25 percent. This can vary somewhat, perhaps at 80 percent to 20 percent or 85 percent to 15 percent; but the point is that one temperature should dominate. Asymmetry in design and color is more interesting than half-warm and half-cool, so it is best not to use 50 percent gold and 50 percent silver in one piece of jewelry. Combining gold and silver also offers more versatility and opportunities for accessorizing. For example, a combination gold and silver bangle bracelet can be worn with either silver or gold bangle earrings and/or necklace.

White, bright freshwater pearls look best against Sunrise colors or complexions, and creamy, natural pearls work best against Sunset colors or complexions. Again, Sunlight people can choose either, depending on the undertones of the colors they are wearing.

Precious stones and gems are so highly reflective that they often blend with or pick up surrounding shadings. Iridescent stones such as opals seem to change according to available light, just as fabrics with a sheen do. Some stones are so definite in their deep, bright, grayed, or honeyed intensity that they look best with other definite Sunrise, Sunlight, or Sunset colors—for example, a dazzlingly bright amethyst with a matching or blending AM tone, or a pinkish cameo tone with soft Midday values. Amber and topaz are usually PM preferences. Let your eye be your guide. At one time grays were only worn with silver. Now we see gold against charcoal and it looks marvelous. Except for a rare or unusual stone, or a very flawed one, diamonds are so highly reflective that they work with everything—the perfect "Crossover" jewel!

NECKLACE: TERESA GOODALL

PHOTO: COURTESY OF 18 KARAT

To really set your personal style, consider having a special piece of jewelry—a ring, bracelet, necklace, pair of earrings—designed incorporating gemstones in your Signature Colors into one unique piece. I worked with a very talented jewelry designer to create a ring that coordinates my Signature Colors, using both silver and gold. This ring goes with everything I own and makes a very personal statement.

CLOTHES TO GO: COLOR PLANNING FOR PACKING

No question about it, one of the biggest color dilemmas is deciding what to take on a trip.

You often pack too much, get the last-minute crazies thinking you have too much, and start to pull things out of the suitcase. Then you get to your destination and wind up buying what you already own (but left at home) because you didn't pack it! We've all done this, and it is frustrating. But it's not impossible to do it right. Organization and lists are key. Make a list of your lists, if necessary; but don't pack without a plan because that's an invitation to color chaos.

Here's how to get started:

- Make a calendar for the days you'll be away. Note the days of your trip and the planned activities for each day. If it's a business trip, you'll know approximately what you will be doing and whom you'll be seeing. Even if it's a trip just for fun and relaxation, you'll know where you are going and what you plan to do when you get there. Of course, you don't have to stick exactly to plan, but at least you'll be covered with enough of the right clothes (literally!).
- List absolutely everything you need for the trip, including pajamas, slippers or socks, undergarments (especially if it's a special bra for a particular top), bathing suits, and cover-ups. Don't leave anything to memory.
- Choose one basic pivotal color. It doesn't have to be black, although black is always a good place to start, especially on a longer trip, where upkeep can be a problem. Don't go to the opposite extreme, either, where you just need a few items for a few days and want to get it all

into a wheelie that you can stash in an overhead bin. Not having to worry about lost luggage is definitely a stress reducer.

- Depending on the length of the trip, your activities, and ease of clothing care, a second basic color can be helpful. If you chose black as the first basic, taupe will work as the second one. You can then wear them together or create entirely different outfits around both.

- It's the blouses, shirts, camisoles, or other tops, scarves, jewelry, and nonbulky sweaters in your Colortime that will give you good alternatives to wear with the basics. They don't take up a lot of space, they're lightweight (a big consideration when your luggage has to be under a certain weight), and they'll keep your basics from getting monotonous, especially if you're seeing the same people every day.

- Leave enough space for outer garments, even in summer or for resort destinations. Hotel and entertainment spots can be frigidly, teeth-chattering cold at any time of the year. Obviously, the basic colors work best; a scarf, cap, or gloves can add color in winter, and all the other accessories add needed color at any time of year.

- Work some of your Signature Colors into your travel plan. This is the time you want to look your very best. Refer to the beginning of this chapter for more details.

- As you pack each item, check it off the list. This will also give you a list of clothes if your luggage gets lost in the friendly skies.

- The last thing to pack is shoes. Whatever your chosen basic, never take just one pair. Even if you choose black as your basic, wear black shoes and pack a pair of black. If your entire wardrobe revolves around one pair of shoes, and it is lost or a heel comes loose (with no shoe repair in sight), you've got a problem.

A Sample Travel Plan: Clothes to Go

The following is a sample color plan for a mix of business and pleasure over a holiday weekend. The vital component is the color thread that connects throughout your stay. This sample starts with the basics and the Crossovers, but if more days are involved (and more fun occasions), you can use additional Colortime shades.

Jewelry in a gold/silver combination is most versatile, worn when appropriate for day or evening and for other fun or dressy pieces. Jewelry and scarves take up so little space and don't add much weight, so always throw in a few extras when you're traveling to spark up your outfits and stretch your wardrobe potential.

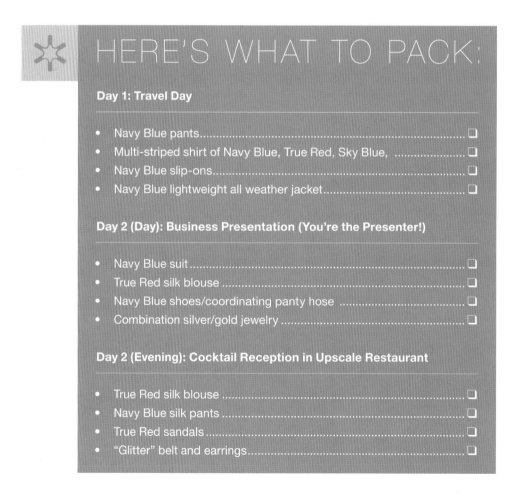

HERE'S WHAT TO PACK:

Day 1: Travel Day

- Navy Blue pants.. ❑
- Multi-striped shirt of Navy Blue, True Red, Sky Blue, ... ❑
- Navy Blue slip-ons.. ❑
- Navy Blue lightweight all weather jacket................................... ❑

Day 2 (Day): Business Presentation (You're the Presenter!)

- Navy Blue suit.. ❑
- True Red silk blouse .... ❑
- Navy Blue shoes/coordinating panty hose .... ❑
- Combination silver/gold jewelry .... ❑

Day 2 (Evening): Cocktail Reception in Upscale Restaurant

- True Red silk blouse .... ❑
- Navy Blue silk pants .... ❑
- True Red sandals .... ❑
- "Glitter" belt and earrings... ❑

THIS SAMPLE STARTS WITH THE BASICS AND THE CROSSOVERS, BUT IF MORE DAYS ARE INVOLVED (AND MORE FUN OCCASIONS), YOU CAN USE ADDITIONAL COLORTIME SHADES

DAY 1 TRAVEL

DAY 2 BUSINESS

DAY 2 EVENING

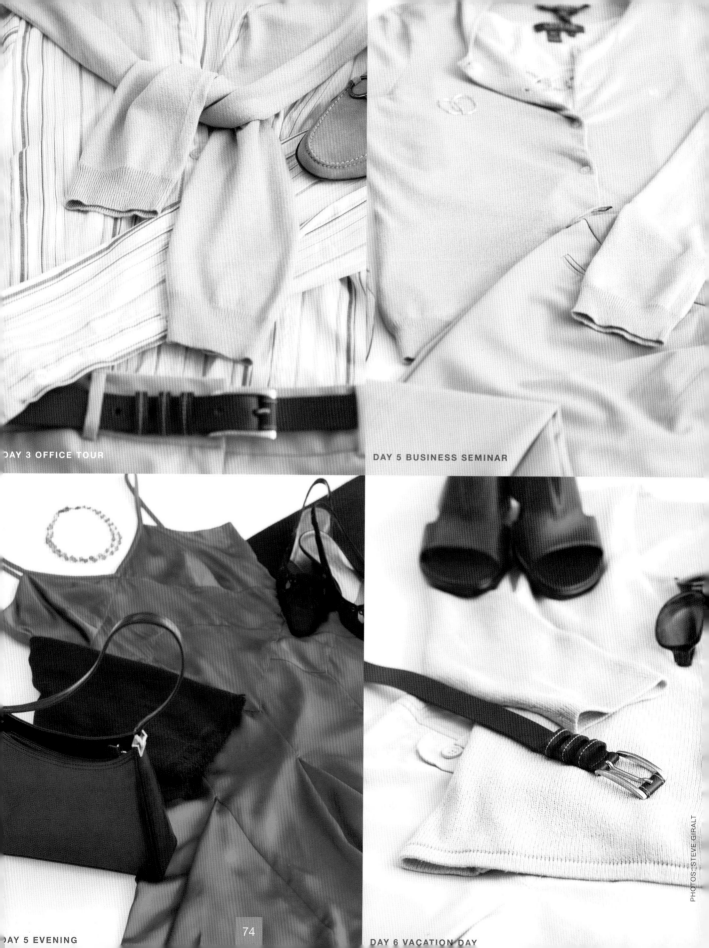

DAY 3 OFFICE TOUR

DAY 5 BUSINESS SEMINAR

DAY 5 EVENING

74

DAY 6 VACATION DAY

Day 3: Office Tour for Clients/Customers: Casual Day

- Light Taupe pants .... ❏
- Multi-stripe shirt of Navy Blue, True Red, Sky Blue......................... ❏
  (worn for travel)
- Sky Blue sweater .... ❏
- Light Taupe flats .... ❏

Day 4: Casual Business Breakfast and Free Day (not shown)

- Denim skirt
- True Red, Sky Blue; Sunlight floral print top .... ❏
- Navy Blue slip-ons.. ❏

Day 5: (Day) Attending Business Seminars

- Light Taupe pants .... ❏
- Sky Blue sweater set .... ❏
- Light Taupe flats .... ❏
- Silver/gold jewelry... ❏

Day 5 (Evening): Dressy Awards Dinner

- Teal silk dress .... ❏
- Beaded necklace of crystals and Teal .... ❏
- Navy Blue wrap... ❏
- Navy Blue heels and bag.. ❏

Day 6: Vacation Day, Not Work-Related

- Bleached Sand shorts and shirt... ❏
- True Red belt .... ❏
- True Red sandals... ❏
- Fun and colorful coordinated jewelry.. ❏

5

INSTANT MAKEOVERS: YOUR COLOR COSMETICS

The Color Clock can save you money by helping you choose the right cosmetic shade every time you buy. As every woman knows, it is easy to accumulate a drawer full of rejects—the makeup base that turned out to be the wrong shade and made you look like you were wearing a mask or the lipstick that looked terrific on your best friend but just didn't make it on you.

Expensive mistakes can add up—a lot of money down the tube, along with the lipsticks. I always recommend trying before buying. Certain shades look totally different on the skin from the way they do in the container. And sometimes a reaction to body chemistry (oiliness, ruddy tones, sallowness, etc.) changes a shade after it has been on the skin for a while.

Always try to buy cosmetics after you've been able to keep them on for a time. Ideally, the products should be applied first, as they are in a demonstration. This is the best way to go—you're unhurried, relaxed, and have a chance to see what the finished product looks like. Try to check yourself in daylight. If that isn't possible, then be sure to use good lighting.

There is nothing mysterious about choosing the correct cosmetic colors; the guidelines that follow can take the guesswork out of it. If you're like most people, you buy too many colors and invariably go back to using your old favorites.

Chances are, these favorites are in your personal Colortime, and that's why you like them. But to help you avoid expensive mistakes (there are no more inexpensive mistakes), remember the pointers on the following page when you choose your most basic cosmetics.

LET YOUR COLORTIME PALETTE GUIDE YOU TO THE BEST COSMETIC COLORS FOR YOU

Points to remember when chosing cosmetics:

1. Every Colortime palette has both warm and cool colors, even though AM tones are predominantly cool, PM tones predominantly warm, and Mid-day a balance of both. You simply need two "sets" of basics—lipstick, blush, and nail polish—one in the warm range of your Colortime and the other in your Colortime's cool tones. If you're in the AM Colortime and use many of the cool colors, you still need a warmer tone to wear with the yellows, some of the warmer pinks, and browns. PM people use up their warm colors first, but they need a cool tone to wear with some of the cooler blues, greens, and purples. Middays are likely to make equal use of their warm and cool tones. If you prefer a gloss or a more "natural" look, seek out a product that blends with your coloring and seems to go with everything.

2. Use your Colortime palette as a guide in choosing your shades. Don't try to match your palette perfectly; simply look for a blend. If your lipstick turns blue no matter what you wear (many people have that problem), try a yellow lipstick under it. If your lips go orange, try a flesh tone as an undercoat.

3. One basic makeup base should blend with your skin tone. Match it as closely as possible so it doesn't look like a mask. You will have to do a lot of experimenting, but it's worth it to get the right shade. Use a colorless, translucent powder over any makeup shade so the base color doesn't change.

4. Eye shadow colors can vary. Your choices include:

- The color of the undertones in your eyes, such as teal shadow with blue-green eyes or amber with brown eyes.

- A complementary color that intensifies the color of your eyes, such as taupe for blue eyes or a dusty rose for green eyes. The color wheel can help you to choose complementary shades, which are suggested by many cosmetic companies. The brightest shade of your "opposite" eye colors on the color wheel will be too intense, so you need to darken or lighten it.

- You may want to match your eye shadow color to your outfit. A very special color, say a dusty lilac, can be accentuated dramatically with a blending eye shadow.

Let your Colortime colors guide your choice of eye shadow colors. Keep your shadow subtle. Dust it down with some taupe or gray so that it shadows, rather than overshadows, your eyes. Basic mascara colors are black or brown-black for dark lashes and dark brown, brown-black, charcoal, or other shades of gray or taupe (depending on the amount of drama you want) for light lashes. Navy is good for blue-eyed people.

There are some color names for each Colortime that will help you make your choices. Of course, shades vary with the manufacturer. These are simply descriptive terms to help you differentiate among the three Colortime palettes. If you have the kind of skin tone that defies every rule, you might have to experiment more than most.

SUNRISE (AM)

Most bases in your Colortime have a very fair or slightly rose-pink, rose-brown, or darkest mahogany undertone. If the base becomes too pink on your skin, go to a straight beige or brown with no discernible undertone and add your color by using blusher on your cheeks, chin, and forehead (just a touch). This is far better than using a shade that is so different from your skin tone that it creates a mask-like line of demarcation.

Sunrise makeup base shades have names like:

Rose-Beige	Rose-Brown	Cool Beige	Mahogany
Light Beige	Fair		

Blushers, rouges, lipsticks, glosses, and nail polishes often have a blue-pink, rose-brown, or cool bluish-wine cast. The name often tells you where to classify the color in the clock.

Typical names include:

Ruby Red	Iced Mauve	Wine and Roses	Porcelain Rose
Seashell	Cherry Brown	Glazed Pink	Frosted Lavender
Pink Icing	Sea Pink		

Adjectives used to describe gems are often a clue to Sunrise shades. They are called "icy," "glistening," "gleaming," "glossy," "glazed," "crystal," "diamond," "sparkling," "frosted," "superfrosted," "silvered," or "brightest."

SUNSET (PM)

PM complexions have a warm undertone. If there is any pink in your skin, it's warm and peachy––not the rosy pink of AM. Honey, cream, and golden are often used as adjectives to describe PM makeup base shades.

Sunset base shades have names like:

Warm Beige	Rachel	Creamy Beige	Deep Tan
Honey Beige	Bronze	Peach	Amber

Sunset blushers, rouges, lipsticks, glosses, and nail polishes have tones of warm pink (such as coral, apricot, or peach), brownish wines, golden brown, and other tawny tones.

Sunset colors may have names like:

Brandied Apricot	Burnished Plum	Copper	Golden Coral
Sienna	Indian Earth	Burnt Almond	Ginger Peachy

Descriptive terms for PM shades include "mellow," "dusky," "honeyed," "golden," "tawny," "brandied," "amber," "burnt," "shadowed," "slate," "coppery," or "heather." They may have a sheen, as in "copper frost," but they are generally "earthier" or "spicier" than AM shades.

SUNLIGHT (MIDDAY)

Sunlight complexions are characterized by a combination of undertones. If you're in this Colortime your best makeup shade is usually a balanced beige with equal amounts of warm and cool undertones.

Sunlight shades are often called:

Natural	Buff	Bisque	Ivory
Medium Beige	Natural Beige	Soft Beige	Basic Beige
Mocha (for slightly darker skin)		Natural Tan (for slightly darker skin)	

When in doubt, try a natural beige tone that blends with your skin and add blusher to cheeks, chin, and forehead.

The Midday colors lean to the subtle, more "natural" look. Eye shadows are best in muted colors or neutral tones.

Sunlight blushers, rouges, lipsticks, glosses, and nail polishes have names like:

Blushing Peach	Gentle Grape	Powder Pink	Cameo Pink
Woodrose	Dusty Lavender	Purple Haze	Mauve Mist

Since Midday colors dip into both of the other two palettes, you can also try the subtler shades from both the AM and PM palettes.

Crossover Colors in cosmetic shades may be used by all palettes. Such shades as Teal, Eggplant (Aubergine), Beaujolais, Seagrass, Light Taupe, and True Red often make beautiful basics. If you're wearing red, but the idea of wearing red lipstick doesn't appeal to you, deepen the color with a bit of brown or outline your lips in red and fill in with a softer shade.

Is it possible to switch from one Colortime to another by changing makeup base shades? Yes, but it's tricky. Since you don't want that line of demarcation where the makeup base ends, it is best to match your skin closely. But if you do want to switch occasionally, blend very carefully at the jaw line by using a slightly dampened sea sponge to carry the color down onto the neck.

You can change your lipstick and blusher to blend with the base. The really tricky part is changing your natural eye color! Colored contact lenses are always an option. If you have hazel eyes, it's less difficult because these are the chameleon shades that tend to reflect the color you wear nearest your face.

Another obstacle to changing Colortimes is hair color. You certainly don't want to change your hair color every other day. When scarves and hats are "in," that's certainly an option. You can fool Mother Nature; it's not impossible, but it is more costly. If you keep switching Colortimes, however, it's best to use coordinating shades in that particular palette.

Models and actresses must make frequent color changes, but wide-ranging makeup shades are part of the tools of their trade. Models' Colortimes often vary for cosmetic ads, but the lighting is changed as well. Since we can't all walk around (unfortunately) with special lights focused on us at all times, it is most flattering to stay in your own Colortime, especially for daytime makeup.

Applying makeup and experimenting with colors can be fun and creative. It's like being a kid again and playing with crayons. Try applying samples of your makeup base, eye colors, lipsticks, and blushers on cardboard (not white paper) to see how a particular group of colors looks together. It's a trick that can help you decide if you like the way they blend and alert you to possible mistakes. As far as disguising those dark circles that can appear from a lack of sleep (or too much partying!), although white cover-up is sometimes recommended, white makeup under the eyes can accentuate circles rather than hide them. Try an off-white or flesh tone instead. Some cover-ups may appear to be a little strange (like orange), but they appear to be flesh-toned when applied.

Most women prefer a few dependable eye shadow colors, a basic makeup and blusher shade, and a few lip colors. Once you have the basics, you can have fun with the extras. And it really is fun to play with new colors. Nothing dates a woman more than an old-fashioned hairstyle or an outmoded lipstick shade. Colorless lips may have been the look in your high school yearbook, but time does march on, and even a touch-up of color does help. It's impossible to have a single lipstick shade that "goes with everything."

You may have trouble finding the right lipstick for "odd" shades. Rather than trying to match a wine sweater that seems to have a brownish undertone, for example, buy a wine shade and blend it with a brownish tone. Or get out some of your rejects (the ones you can't bring yourself to throw away) and try them with a new color. See how inventive and creative you can be. A word of caution—be careful of intensely purpled or very blue-based lipsticks if your teeth are yellowed. Soften the blue undertone or warm it up slightly.

For those of you who are "naturalists" and refer to makeup as unnatural, think of cosmetics as a protective covering for the skin (which they are as the ozone layer diminishes). Think of color as cosmetic enhancement. It truly can help you look more alive with color!

6

HAIR INSPIRATION: YOUR COLORS COUNT

If you color your hair, choosing the right shade can be more confusing than choosing cosmetics. The name of the color will generally give you a good idea of whether it is AM, Midday, or PM—Arctic Blonde (AM), Honey Blonde (PM), and Neutral Blonde (Midday), for example. The photo on the box or in an illustrated brochure can be a fairly good indicator of the color inside. Many terms sound delicious but can be difficult to classify: "Sweet Meringue" or "Double Latté." However, there is usually a description of the color on the box or on product websites that tells you whether it's warm, cool, or neutral, so it's best to do some homework before shopping.

Professional hair product companies advise you to choose your hair coloring shades based on what is called "tonality," the warmth or coolness of a color. Cool tones are called ash tones, while warm is defined as golden or red tones. They also allow for a third category that is not clearly defined and call it "neutral." Although it's a very broad definition, it's very similar to the Colortime concept.

Body chemistry, however, can affect hair, just as it does cosmetics. Your hair may have a natural red or gold tone that has a tendency to come through whatever color you use. You may find this an attractive undertone, especially if you have PM coloring. But if you want to play down the red-gold, use a product with either cool or ash undertones.

Conversely, if you have used a product that gave your hair a green or blue-green tinge, a reddish shade can help to neutralize the blue-green. If you are blonde or gray and have used a product that added unwanted violet or silver, a golden shade is a good neutralizer. Strange things can happen to your skin tone if your hair coloring clashes with your Colortime. Hair is a crucial part of your self-image, and it's well worth the time it takes to get the color right.

If this seems totally confusing, not to worry. Your local beauty supply store can advise you, or your hairdresser can help. If you've really made a mess, let a professional undo the damage. Limit your experiments with new colors to small strands of hair until you are sure of how the color will respond to you.

The following guidelines can help you with hair color choices; and your Colortime can be a tremendous help. Your natural color is never wrong, but if you want to change it, cover it up, or enhance it, use the shades that will appear most natural.

If your hairstylist does your coloring, please introduce him or her to the use of Colortimes. Hairstylists can do a fantastic job on color without it, if they have a good eye for color. But because not all hairstylists are colorists, they may be tempted to choose a color simply because it's in their Colortime—not yours!

COLOR NAMES VARY DEPENDING ON THE MANUFACTURER; USE THE FOLLOWING AS A GENERAL GUIDE

If you are an AM blonde, ash or platinum tones blend best with your skin. A bit of yellow is all right, but brassy gold will not blend with your cool skin. You want to eliminate as much gold as possible.

Sunrise Blonde

Sunrise: Shades that most closely describe Sunrise blondes have names like:

| Ash Blonde | Nordic | Sheer Diamond | Platinum |
| Cool Blonde | Star Light | | |

If you are in a sunny climate, your hair tends to turn a yellow-gold. As a PM blonde, this is not a bad thing, because golden undertones blend with your skin and hair and look terrific and natural.

Sunset Blonde

Sunset: In choosing hair colors, PM blondes look for such key words as:

| Warm Blonde | Warm Beige | Golden Blonde | Honey Blonde |
| Light Amber | | | |

Sunlight Blonde

Sunlight

If you are a Midday blonde, a combination of blonde shades can be very effective. Because you tend to have variety in your natural color, and your skin has both warm and cool undertones, variegated hair can be extremely flattering. Highlighting is especially good on Middays, and shades from the AM and PM palette can be combined. If the hair coloring product is described as "neutral," it will generally work for you.

REDHEADS

The term, redhead, covers a wide range of colors. True auburn tends to flatter AM skins, because it has a relatively cool cast compared with the rust-copper undertones of a golden PM red. Sunrise reds are rarer than Sunset reds. Their really fair skin is a good "clue." PM redheads with sallow or yellowed skin should be wary of intensifying golden tones, which may emphasize their sallowness; a mixture of cooler auburn mixed with coppery shades might work better than straight copper for these skin colors, as the auburn tones can help to cool down the sallowness.

Red hair may also have a tendency to become "brassy." Regardless of your Colortime, be careful of harsh tones if your skin is aging or sallow. You may have to switch to a less vivid color to keep the brassiness out.

Sunrise: AM red shades have names like:

Sherry	Plum	Ruby	Berry
Dark Auburn	Medium Auburn	Light Auburn	

Sunrise Red

Sunset: PM red shades are apt to be called:

Coppertone	Red Penny	Rich Copper	Sun Bronze
Honey Red	Spicy Ginger	Reddish Blonde	Burnished Copper

Sunset Red

Sunlight

Midday redheads are never bright. If you're a redheaded Midday, your color is more subtle and often streaked. Combined auburn and copper tones are a good choice. In many instances, natural redheads go from AM or PM to Midday when their hair begins to be streaked with gray. As you get older, softer hair shades are more flattering than bright or deep tones that look great surrounding a flawless complexion.

Sunlight Red

Redheads in every Colortime should be careful of fiery reds and neon oranges in clothing because they may compete or clash with their hair and overshadow it. If you're a PM redhead who loves these colors, use them as accents, prints, or in a solid shade away from the hair. Tawny shades like terra cotta, peach, warm chocolate browns, and apricot are better to use near your hair than are brilliant orange reds, AM auburns, with their cool red tones, look wonderful in shades of rose pinks, dark mahogany, and eggplant. Midday redheads are terrific in peaches and cream, custard yellow, powdery pinks, and hazy or jade-like greens.

AM browns usually have ash undertones, which may range from quite light to very dark. If a red tone is present, it is auburn- or berry-colored.

Sunrise Brown

Sunrise Sunrise brown shades are often described as:

Light Ash Brown	Dark Ash Brown	Icy Brown	Rich Sable
Medium Ash Brown			

PM browns tend to accent amber tones.

Sunset Brown

Sunset: Colors in this range (from lightest to darkest undertones) are often called:

Warm Brown	Honeyed Brown	Bronze	Caramel
Golden Brown	Russet	Tawny Brown	

Sunlight

Midday browns are variegated combinations of warm and cool tones. The most natural-looking combination combines both the AM and PM Color-time shades, and professional stylists often combine warm and cool tones to get just the right balance.

Sunlight Brown

Once upon a time, all little gray-haired ladies put blue rinses on their hair. Golden tones in gray were a definite no-no. In spite of the trend to more natural graying, most gray hair coloring products continue to boast that they "get the yellow out" as though it were some sort of dreaded affliction!

If you are a PM, let the yellow stay in. Nature intended for your hair to blend with your skin and eyes. If your skin is sallow, you may want to liven up the gray somewhat by giving it sheen, which can be done with a good conditioner, or you may want to go to a warm gray rinse. These are more difficult to find than the cool AM shades, and their names are often mis-

Sunlight Gray

leading. Some "Snow Whites" and "Pearly Whites" are in the warm range. You simply have to experiment.

The cool silvery tones of an AM gray are very striking, but an AM really should try to keep the color from going too yellow. Try a good conditioner in your natural color. If this doesn't do it, there are lots of good AM grays on the market, with names like "Silver," "Cool White," and "Silver Diamond." Gray and white hair, like blonde, tends to yellow in sunlight. If you are an AM gray, remember to protect your hair from bright sunlight.

The term, salt and pepper, describes those who are changing from their natural darker color to gray. The emerging gray of AM people shows a silvery or pure white tone. A pewter gray mixture is characteristic of PMs, and the graying hair of Middays tends to have both warm and cool tones. Middays look great with salt and pepper or mixed grays as you have a natural inclination to a mix of variegated tones in your hair.

Some people begin to "go gray" at a very early age, even as young as their twenties. Coloring your hair is a very personal choice. If you feel old with graying hair, and that makes you uncomfortable, by all means cover it up. But use your Colortime recommendations so it looks "natural."

Sunset Gray

Sunlight Gray

BLACKS

True blue-black is always AM. This is why tinted blue-black hair can look so phony on some people. They are Midday or PM, and it simply does not go with their skin and eyes. This can make tinted black hair painfully obvious—more so than any other color. This is especially true for men, because they lack cosmetics to help their skin tones blend with the tinted shade.

It's also very difficult to retain blue-black hair as you grow older, because it can be so harsh next to yellowing or aging skin. I always suggest a dark cool brown or a brown mixed with a smidgen of black for "maturing" AMs, a mixture of medium to dark browns for Middays, and a dark honey-eyed brown for PMs.

Blue-black really does look best on flawless, fair, or youthful AM skin. The natural hair color of black-haired PMs, as dark as it may seem, is often closer to deep brown or umber brown-black rather than blue-black. There is no black in the Sunlight palette.

Sunrise Black

Sunset Black

7

FOR MEN ONLY

Many areas of a man's wardrobe give him the chance to experience the fun and creativity of color. Workout clothes and sportswear, casual tops and robes, and knit shirts come in every color of the rainbow. When men know their Colortime, they can use the same shades as their female counterparts do when they are relaxing and in some creative jobs. But despite having more freedom in dress and clothing colors than ever before, men may still need to dress conservatively for certain types of business.

I find that the best colors for a man to build a business wardrobe around are the Crossover Colors. They work for all palettes and have enough variety to keep a wardrobe from getting dull. You can always spark it up with a shirt in your own palette like a soft mauve, light lavender, or deep peach. But you can stay within the framework of the most basic Crossover Colors and have a very workable, acceptable wardrobe.

The staples, of course, include the Crossover Colors of Charcoal and Neutral Gray, Light Taupe, Navy Blue, Jet Black, and variations of brown, such as Dark Earth and Cappuccino, Beaujolais (Wine), Eggplant (Aubergine), Pineneedle, Seagrass, and Pale Khaki. Sunlight, Teal, and True Red can be used as accent colors in ties and handkerchiefs. Light Taupe, Neutral Gray, Sky Blue, Faded Denim, Seagrass, Pale Khaki, Teal, and Bleached Sand make excellent shirt colors, both as solids and in combinations. And, depending on trends and/or appropriateness, deeper colors are dramatic and compelling in shirts.

The Crossovers are also the source of "Power" colors, which you'll learn about in chapter 8. Since the Crossover Colors work for all palettes, I usually suggest suit and/or jacket colors on the basis of hair color. Gray and navy are excellent with gray, black, blonde, or silver hair, as are variations of brown with brown and red hair.

Personal Signature Colors are often the source of shirt and/or tie color.

The most common mistakes made in coordinating a business wardrobe are:

- Too Monochromatic—Light gray suit, pale blue shirt, pale blue tie
- Too Many Directional Patterns—Plaids, stripes, and patterns, each headed in a different direction
- Wrong Mood—Sporty shirt with business suit
- Wrong Texture—Light, summery, silky tie with wintry wool suit or jacket
- Wrong Colors—Too many colors from opposite Colortimes

When in doubt, these are the combinations that always work:

- Solid suit, patterned shirt, solid tie
- Solid suit, patterned tie, solid shirt
- Solid suit, solid shirt, solid tie (only if one element is colorful or contrasting, for example, Navy Blue suit, Sky Blue shirt, and Beaujolais tie.

Other possible combinations for men include:

- A solid suit with a patterned shirt and patterned tie if one is nondirectional or has a subtle pattern or colors—for example, a solid gray suit with a light gray and white pinstripe shirt and a tie in a small paisley print of soft colors, including gray. The tie always looks coordinated when its pattern includes the colors of the suit and/or shirt.
- A rep tie is acceptable with a striped shirt because it is traditional. Your eye is accustomed to this combination, and diagonal lines are neither vertical nor horizontal. But the colors and textures must blend.
- Wear a solid shirt and solid tie with a patterned suit, such as a glen plaid—for example, a gray glen plaid suit with a light gray shirt and medium gray tie. If the plaid is very muted, a solid shirt with a subtly patterned tie is possible.
- A pinstripe suit looks best with a solid shirt and tie, but you can use a tie with a subtle pattern—for example, a navy pinstripe suit with a white shirt and a navy and white tie in a small polka dot. If the pinstripe is hardly discernible, a narrow-stripe shirt is possible, but with a solid tie. It's best to wear solids with tweeds to keep from looking too "busy."

If you don't have a good eye for combinations, or you simply want to play it safe, don't put two patterns together. Pick up the colors of the suit or shirt in the tie.

For conservative business wear, shirt patterns should be low-key and subtle. Against a pale background, such colors as brown, wine, gray, dark blue, and even black can work in a patterned shirt. However, bright colors, such as red, orange, purple, or bright pinks, even when they are part of a trend, have to be handled with care as they can be construed as too eccentric or over the top. They can be great for sportswear, or in the "glamour" industries, but not for a conventional business look.

A touch of brightness sparks a dark tie. Pure white or a dab of color can lift a dark suit, but the area should be small and restricted to the pattern, not the background. Solids and small patterns are best, such as small polka dots, narrow stripes, small geometrics, miniature plaids, and subtle paisleys. In general, the fewer the colors, the more formal the tie. A colored or patterned silk square in the breast pocket can be added for a touch of color, but it should relate to the tie color. When they are in style, vests can provide a good "pulled together" look. Not only do they disguise a midsection in need of a workout, but when the vest and pants match, the body appears taller and slimmer.

PHOTO: COURTESY OF PAUL FREDRICK'S MENSWEAR

Shoes and Socks

Some fashion authorities feel that men's socks should match, blend, or relate to tie color—for example, a red and silver grey striped tie with deep wine socks. Bright red socks are a bit much, and again, a little affected, eccentric, or weird. Wine is a better choice; it's related to the red in the tie and far less obvious. Another example is a sky blue and taupe tie with navy socks. Sky blue is related to navy, and light blue socks are inappropriate. Light socks give a casual look to an outfit, so they aren't right for business or dress wear. I feel that you're always "safe" with the darkest sock colors. If you're not wearing a tie, your socks should match your shoes.

If you're a conventional dresser or work in a conservative industry, black and brown are your best shoe shades. But if you like to experiment or you're in a "glamour" industry, try the neutral shoe colors, especially in warm climates or weather or for sportswear. Remember, lighter neutrals work only with lighter-color clothing.

WHERE YOU LIVE CAN COLOR YOUR STYLE

Colors vary according to geographical location. Generally, the farther north and east you go, the more conservative the look and the color. Washington, D.C., Boston and environs, and New York (especially in the financial world) are considered to be among the most conservative. Dark suits and light shirts are the general rule. Minneapolis and other Midwestern areas share the "East Coast" look.

Colors and patterns in suits are lighter and more relaxed in the South and West. Medium-range tans, khaki, and grays are safe suit colors in these regions. A sandy beige or taupe suit is acceptable in summer in all areas.

Los Angeles is relaxed and often trendy; top executives in most industries, however, are often dressed conservatively. Texas and other areas of the Southwest also have their own special look. It's okay for natives to wear big ten-gallon Stetsons and pointed boots with business suits, but if you're an outsider and affect that look, you'll look just like that—an outsider.

As we all know, casual dressing for business is permissable in many (but not all) businesses today. If not every day, than generally one day of the week. The color and style rules are (literally) more relaxed ... more about that in chapter 8.

Regardless of style, casual or more businesslike (or dressy), your Colortime colors always help you to look and feel your best.

Many men color their hair, for many of the same reasons women do: they want to look better and improve their self-image. But please remember that gray or white hair can be very attractive and appealing. Look at some of the men in male magazines who have "gone gray." They certainly don't look like your grandfather!

Be warned, however, if you color your hair, you must commit to keeping it up. New growth of the unwanted color looks obvious and unkempt. A slight "highlighting" is often better than a solid shade, because new growth is far less obvious, and you can go for a longer time without recoloring. It's also best for men to stay with subtle colors. Please, no severe blue-blacks after thirty! It looks like shoe polish on the head, and the starkness draws attention to less-than-youthful skin.

As we age, our skin picks up lines, wrinkles, and yellow pigment, and it may become spotty. Thus, hair color should be "softer" to deemphasize these changes. Don't try to duplicate the exact shade of hair that you had at age fifteen in high school. A hair color that looks great on a teen can be pushing it at age fifty.

IF YOU WANT TO FEEL BETTER ABOUT YOURSELF, OR IF YOUR GRAYING HAIR MAKES YOU FEEL OLDER, USE THE GUIDELINES IN CHAPTER 6. THEY APPLY TO YOU, TOO.

part 2

what color says about you

8

USING COLOR
TO INFLUENCE OTHERS

Color is a very effective form of communication, and we
say a lot about ourselves through the colors we wear
and use. In this chapter you'll learn how to use color
as a powerful tool in getting your message across and
establishing your style. Let's start with your personality.

Circle the words below that you feel reflect your personality.

EXTROVERT	INTROVERT
ANIMATED	QUIET
INTENSE	RELAXED
REALISTIC	IDEALISTIC
FORCEFUL	GENTLE
DRAMATIC	RESERVED
DIRECT	SUBTLE
ACTIVE	PASSIVE
ANALYTICAL	INTUITIVE
ASSERTIVE	SUBMISSIVE
EXUBERANT	CALM

YANG OR YIN?

The words listed above are divided into two columns because they are opposites. The words on the left describe "yang" traits; those on the right are "yin" traits. The yang is thought to be more forceful and active, the yin more gentle or passive.

The terms come from the ancient Chinese, who believed that each person is a blend of two personalities, the yang and the yin. These opposite characteristics, when put together, make up the whole, balanced person.

How much of your personality is yang and how much is yin? Look at the descriptive words you circled in each category. Add up your yangs and your yins. Did you circle more traits in one column than in the other?

Nearly everyone is a composite of both, because within the frame-work of your "type," your moods may change. The tiger in the outside world may be a kitten at home (or vice versa!). Colors have personalities, too. Every Colortime has both yang and yin colors. You simply vary the shadings according to the mood you want to convey.

If you want to express a yin mood, use the light to medium colors. If you want to express a yang mood, use the more vibrant or darker colors. Every hue ranges in mood from yin through yang. The lightest reds are pink. They are yin-soft, easy, non-threatening. As the pinks get closer to the

Each person is a blend of both yin and yang personality traits that together make up the whole, balanced you.

Every hue ranges in mood from yin to yang, from light to dark.

"mother color," red, they take on more yang characteristics. The brighter reds are attention-getting dynamic yangs. The deeper wine-reds carry more authority and weight. They are also yang, but with added dignity.

You may not be aware that you are expressing a mood when you choose the colors of the clothing you wear, but you really are. Have you ever tried shopping on a day when you're not feeling too good about yourself? If you're feeling down, it's difficult to come home with anything in a color that you like. Try to do your shopping on a day when you are feeling "up." But if you can't always plan it that way, take your Colortime palette with you to avoid mistakes.

Wearing light or mid-tone colors—or deep or vibrant colors—all the time can get monotonous. Just as you try to keep a balance in your personality, you should work toward balance in your clothing choices, too. The words that you circle might change from month to month or even from day to day, depending on what's going on in your life.

Nothing can signal a change of personality to the rest of the world more quickly than a change of colors. One of my clients had been dodging marriage to his fiancée for about five years. Coincidentally, she worked with another of my clients and told me that she had had enough of this long-standing relationship with no engagement ring in sight. She was ready to make some changes in her life, but she needed a little encouragement.

I recommended that she start by bringing some pretty peach or violet tones into her Sunlight palette to replace or liven up the light grays and beiges she often wore. She had lovely hazel eyes with flecks of blue-green in them. I suggested Blue Turquoise, a color she had never worn before, to enhance her eye color. She had always used pale aquas—pretty for lingerie and soft summer dresses—but she needed more pizzazz for her new color personality.

I also suggested that she weave several blonde shades, ash and gold-beige, into her mousey-brown hair to get some color variation next to her skin.

You've probably guessed the end of the story. They were married in a matter of months ... she in a turquoise dress, he in a gray suit (with a turquoise tie). He said he knew his days were numbered when she started to add more yang touches to her wardrobe!

At one time, yang traits were considered exclusively masculine, and yin characteristics were women's territory. Today we are less apt to classify color meanings by sex. Men are less reluctant to reveal their gentler side, and women less afraid to exhibit assertiveness. Men wear pastel pink shirts and still come across as very masculine, and women wear dark, tailored pants without losing their femininity.

Yang and yin colors can be combined. This is more difficult than staying with just one mood, but, again, the secret is balance. For women, a Charcoal Gray business suit in a very tailored mood can be softened by a lavender camisole. The suit is yang; the cami is yin. It is true that most male styles are yang, but occasionally some yin breaks through. I have seen many macho types on formal evenings with ruffled yin pastel dress shirts under their yang black tuxedos. Can you imagine those he-man types ever wearing a ruffled shirt with a pair of jeans? Yet it's perfectly acceptable for formal wear. These shirts are probably the last holdovers from the days of powdered wigs and satin waistcoats.

The yang navy blazer can be worn with a light blue shirt for a touch of yin contrast. When you change colors to suit your changing moods, be sure your choice is appropriate for the occasion. An Electric Green T-shirt may be great on a golf course, but all wrong in a dignified courtroom.

You may feel that some physical liability limits the colors you can wear. Don't let the fact that you're heavier than you'd like to be commit you to a life of the "blahs." You don't have to wear dark yang colors all the time to reflect your yang moods—add a touch of brightness from your palette, preferably close to the face, to give you a spark.

Shy or reserved people often have trouble handling the brighter yang shades for obvious reasons. But color can work to your advantage if you're shy—use a touch of a bright yang color and people will be drawn to you. At a party, you won't have to break the ice first—someone else will, because colors work like a magnet to draw others to you.

I had a client once say to me, "I'm a yang personality in a tiny yin body and my yang is dying to get out!" If you're a little person with a dynamic personality, you can relate to that. Being short or petite is no reason to avoid vivid colors, especially if you're outgoing. If vibrancy is part of your personality, vibrant colors reflect who you are. And even if you're a Sunlight with a penchant for more subtle or neutral tones, a touch of Crossover True Red or a sunny yellow can really reflect your friendly and gregarious disposition.

The dynamic yang colors of this classic handbag make it a glamorous accessory.

Because dress codes have relaxed, and the debate continues about whether they are getting a bit too relaxed, a lot of attention has been paid recently to color in clothing for business. For business wear, the basic yang colors carry more weight and convey an aura of power and authority. The most powerful colors for men are navy, dark brown, dark or medium gray, taupe, and, of course, black, which has become a real designer statement in its sleek simplicity.

At one point, there was a hint of country associated with brown. Although brown is dark and dependable and as solid as the earth, some men in large cosmopolitan areas stayed away from it because they didn't feel it was urban enough. They used it in leather or suede, but not in a suit or jacket. Currently, brown, especially in the darker espresso shades, has become more mainstream for both casual and business wear.

Women have also accepted brown as more elegant than ever. Think polished leather, supple suedes, and, yes, even chocolate diamonds!

Women have a greater color range to use in expressing power.

The most powerful Crossover basic shades are:

JET BLACK	NAVY BLUE	NEUTRAL GRAY	CHARCOAL GRAY
LIGHT TAUPE	BLEACHED SAND	SEAGRASS	PINENEEDLE
BEAUJOLAIS	EGGPLANT	CAPPUCCINO	TEAL
DARK EARTH	PALE KHAKI		

You will find additional power colors in your Colortime. Just remember that the darker mid to deep "yang" shades are the best source of power colors.

The lighter neutrals of sand, light taupes, grays, and khakis are not as powerful for either sex as the deeper values are, but they are appropriate substitutes during the summer or in warm climates. A word of caution about summer-weight fabrics: it's more of a challenge to look powerful in clothes that looked "slept in." So stick with those that stay crisp. Power colors can be combined with your signature colors, such as a taupe suit with a patterned tie or blouse that contains your hair, skin, and eye color.

When I started my color consulting business, I did corporate seminars on suitable clothing for businessmen and women. The president of a large company called me in to try to upgrade the image of his sales force. His particular problem was that most of his salespeople were accustomed to the casual Los Angeles lifestyle, and their clothing colors were just not credible for selling a prestige service, especially in conservative northeastern states.

A few of the men were resistant to change (the women were not), but most of them were receptive to changing their wardrobes to the more powerful, deeper tones. Their sales increased along with their credibility.

When I first moved to Los Angeles from the East Coast, I was hired by a large Beverly Hills department store as a member of its executive staff. I wore many hats, including keeping the employees and the departments looking chic and up-to-date and producing fashion shows.

Before I got the job, I had become so enamored of Southern California's sunshine and lifestyle that I bought lots of colorful new clothes to go along with my new life. I packed all of my dark basics—black, navy, browns, grays, etc.—off to a friend in New York.

When I was hired by the corporate personnel director, she told me that the required dress code consisted of what she considered credible colors. You guessed it: black, navy, browns, and grays, and taupe and beige were acceptable in summer. Even in casual California, authority carries more weight in darker colors.

There's no question that basic colors are the most practical. Some colors come and go, depending on fashion's whim, but basics are here forever. They are the dependable, serviceable standbys.

But basics can get boring, so for business wear I suggest some color near the face. For men, a touch of color in the tie or shirt; for women a sweater, blouse, or sparkling jewelry or a scarf in a becoming color that radiates into the face can add just the right impact. Which colors are your impact colors? The hues in your Colortime that are your true favorites—and the most becoming.

REMEMBER THAT THE DARKER MID TO DEEP "YANG" SHADES ARE THE BEST SOURCE OF POWER COLORS

Try something different in combinations of power colors. Instead of the cliché look of a brown suit with a beige blouse, try a brown suit with a lavender or violet blouse or a navy suit with a fresh spring green blouse. The basic suit conveys the power, and the impact color is used next to the face.

Men, unfortunately, are much more limited than women in their color choices, but there are ways to break the sameness habit. Navy blazers are great basics, but why not try a shirt in Crossover Seagrass or another color from your Colortime, Crossover Neutral Gray slacks, and a tie that contains all three colors? The power of navy is predominant, but Seagrass adds a welcome creative touch.

Study the colors in your preferred Colortime. Stretch your imagination and look for new combinations. The simplest method for finding interesting color combinations is to line up all of your colors and start playing with various possibilities. This will open you up to new and colorful ways of thinking, and it is really a very creative exercise.

Turn to your Colortime palette and take it with you when you go shopping. You can't remember a color exactly when walk even three feet away from it. You might get lucky and make the right choice, but then again, you might not. After it's been cut off the bolt or if it's on "final sale," right or wrong, it's yours forever (or at least until you finally give it away!).

Chapter 3 gave you the basics of color combinations and ideas about how to use colors together. If you need help in combining colors, refer to the Goof-Proof combinations as a guide.

Power colors have been used effectively in uniforms for many years. Dark blue is the most universal of all uniform colors—it connotes all of the dependable messages of blue, but with the added strength and solemnity of the blackened undertone. In many areas, tans and khakis are issued in summer to replace the traditional dark blue policeman's uniforms. Although lighter in color, they still connote a military look and suggest aggressive action if necessary. A head-to-toe black uniform can be forbidding and scary—a bit too "Darth Vaderish"—creating fear rather than inspiring confidence. Black is more acceptable as a uniform when it's trimmed with gold braid and worn with a white shirt to "purify" the darkness. A black sweater, jacket, and slacks can be very smart (and slimming) on a man; "civilian" clothes are always a bit less imposing than uniforms.

The psychological message of a uniform seems to inspire consumer confidence. Airlines have long recognized the importance of inspiring the confidence of passengers by keeping flight crews in darker power colors. In the psychedelic '60s, some airlines deviated by dressing female flight attendants in cutesy miniskirts and garish color combinations, but that

stopped when the women's movement started. How can a passenger have confidence in a Barbie doll? Although there is some relaxation in color choices today, especially for holiday destinations and more casual dressing, for the most part, airline uniforms are still in power colors.

In general, the nursing profession has veered away from sterile whites into pastels. These color ranges are seen as friendlier and more approachable. If you wear a uniform to work and are given a choice, go for the colors in your Colortime. If you don't have a choice, then changing into "your" colors will have to wait until you get home.

CASUAL DRESSING IN THE OFFICE

Fashion has come a long way from the rigidly prescribed rules of the past. If you can believe it, women once never dreamed of wearing pants to the office, and men always wore a white shirt and conservative dark tie. White shoes were only worn from Memorial Day to Labor Day, and anyone who broke those rules was committing a fashion faux pas.

Now most women wear pants more often than they wear skirts, shirts are worn in all kinds of colors and patterns, collars come in a variety of styles or are missing completely, and ties are almost an endangered fashion species. We have a new attitude, called "fashion freedom."

But all is not well in Fashion Freedomland. As is true in every democracy, some people abuse their privileges. It's gotten so bad that a national magazine ran a cover story begging the question, "Have we become a nation of slobs?" Network television has run pictures of people in some really tacky states of dress (or undress) that are inappropriate for the office.

But most upstanding citizens have good intentions, and even though they don't want to go back to the days of fashion dictatorship, they are looking for guidelines (a much more democratic word than rules).

When in doubt, think simple, tailored, and classic style and wear your Signature Colors (see chapter 4) for more interesting, personalized looks. For example, belts and shoes can be in basic colors like black or brown, but when you feel a dressier or more fun look is in order, add some colorful touches.

The basic principles of dressing casually and looking professional for women are very similar. Build a wardrobe around a few basic pieces that you can wear in different ways, such as a black or khaki skirt or pants, a jacket in black or neutral colors, twin sweater sets, cotton knit shirts in colors, and small to medium-size prints in pants, skirts, or tops. If it's too short, too bare, too tight (or too baggy), it's too much (or not enough) for the office, no matter how "casual" the dress code.

Leave the loud, busy prints; oversize jewelry; and short, short skirts for after five, weekends, or vacations. Panty hose or leg makeup really look neater in air-conditioned offices, and unless you're willing to invest in pedicures, shoes shouldn't be too open and bare. (For basic guides in accessorizing with color, see chapter 4.) Again, your Signature Colors will help to customize or glamorize your look, as appropriate.

The question of jeans and denim in the office depends entirely on company policy. In many businesses, denim is allowed on at least one day. In others the dress code is very loose, the business does not rely on any formality at all, and everyone is relaxed about the idea of jeans or other denim apparel.

If you're a denim lover and feel comfortable in denim clothing of all kinds, from jeans to jackets, you really need to find out about the dress code. If you're the casual type who can't tolerate the thought of more standard business attire, then you might need to make this a priority when considering a job. Ask the right questions before you go on the job interview. Check out the office before the interview, if possible, to get an accurate picture of what is acceptable. The worst mistake is showing up for the interview in more standard dress and then switching to something too casual when you start working. It looks as if you were playing a role at the job interview and then decided to flout the rules by wearing whatever pleases you afterward.

If you work in a home office, there is no problem ever, unless you see clients in your office or you venture out to their offices. Then the same guidelines apply. People still think that sloppy clothes equal sloppy work— not a good message if you want to keep their business.

PEOPLE STILL THINK THAT SLOPPY CLOTHES EQUAL SLOPPY WORK, NOT A GOOD MESSAGE IF YOU WANT TO KEEP THEIR BUSINESS.

Here are some good "rules" to follow:

- Wear jeans that fit well, nothing too tight, too baggy, or too low.
- Professionalize the look by adding a leather belt and leather shoes in black, brown, or burgundy wines.
- Sweater sets, fitted jackets, and blazers also dress up jeans.
- Neatness counts, so jeans should be clean. Leave the paint-spattered or bleach-spotted jeans at home for after work.
- Don't wear distressed looks, novelty dye jobs, sparkle, or studs to the office.
- Denim jackets also work with khakis, over casual dresses, and with skirts.
- Wear the skirt at a length that flatters your leg. Again, too short is too casual and not for the office.
- Darker denims are even more professional, especially if they're in a suede finish.

SURFACE LANGUAGE: YOUR FIRST IMPRESSION

You never have another chance to make a first impression. Color can help you make that initial meeting something special. We often want to make a special first impression, especially on social occasions, but the most important occasion is likely to be a job interview. Experts tell us about the four-minute time barrier, a period during which initial human contact is established. If the initial reaction is negative, the eye and the mind start to wander elsewhere.

When you're at a party and introduce yourself to a stranger, you begin a conversation. The first four minutes are spent evaluating each other. We all do it, whether we admit it or not. You do start to make judgments based on what you see, since it doesn't take an expert to tell us that the styles and colors that people wear attract or repel us. As superficial as that may seem, if you want to get beyond the four-minute evaulation, first impressions do count, so dress not only to please your self-image, but to also broadcast to others. Our taste is a vital clue to our personalities.

Although you may be asked to take an aptitute test (or any other test appropriate to the job), there is always that "unwritten" test that plays an important role in landing a job. Personnel interviewers also judge you by your verbal, body, and surface language. To anyone going on an interview, I always make the following suggestions about color to make that initial contact successful.

How to dress for a job interview

1. Every business has a collective personality. Wear colors that are appropriate for that business. Obviously, a conservative power color like navy or gray works best for an interview with a top-level industry, attorney, or accounting office.

2. If you're going for a job with a glamour industry, women can (and should) wear trendy shades to accent power colors. You'll demonstrate to a prospective employer that you know what's happening in the fashion field. Men can bring interesting colors into shirts and ties. Don't wear something unimaginative like a white shirt and a solid tie.

3. As stylish as it may be, men should avoid an all-black look for some conservative companies. In the companies' eyes, you'll look like something out of an old Mafia movie—too gangsterish and slick or too GQ, especially for banking, insurance, and accounting firms.

4. Chances are you're one of many applicants. Try to make yourself a little more memorable by using some interesting, colorful conversation piece. For women, this is easy—an interesting piece of jewelry, a trendy scarf, or an impact color in your blouse can help make you stand out from the other applicants. For men, a colorful tie or shirt has to suffice, preferably in your Signature Colors.

5. Avoid colors that are generally turnoffs or "tacky" brilliant—overly vivid purples, brilliant oranges, garish yellow-greens, for example. Wear those colors and you'll be memorable, but for the wrong reasons.

Your anxiety level is high on a job interview, so you want to wear colors that make you feel confident, and confidence-building colors are those that make you look and feel your best. For that reason, I recommend wearing your Signature Colors—those that repeat, contrast, and/or enhance your personal coloring. For example, if you have AM ash blonde hair, deep blue eyes, and fair pinkish skin, your best Signature Colors are a Frost Gray suit with a Bonnie Blue turtleneck or shirt. If you wear a small scarf, it can include frosty tones and vibrant blue, both of which are flattering to your hair and eyes. Adding a touch of contrasting rose tone, such as Prism Pink, will enhance your complexion color (as rose and pink always do, regardless of skin tone). A man can substitute a tie for the scarf in the very same colors. And please don't think of the pink or rose tones as too "girly"—take a look at some of the fabulously fashionable men's ties and shirts today.

If you have Midday brown hair highlighted with blonde streaks; hazel eyes that change to blue, green, and brown; and variegated skin tones of rose-beige, you have lots of options. A sand-colored suit will show off your hair color (and complement your skin); add a blue-green shirt for your eyes, and a tie or scarf of sand and blue-green with a touch of dusty rose. These are your Signature Colors—a wonderful way to capitalize on your own coloring and make you stand out from the crowd.

If you have a deep mocha PM skin tone, warm amber eyes, and honey brown hair, it's easy to see that golden tawny tones like Camel or Cognac will be wonderful on you. A coral pink necklace will brighten your skin and add a great accent.

COLORS FOR PRESENTATIONS

Naturally, the type of presentation that you are doing, the location, and the audience have a lot to do with the choice. Are you presenting to a glamour industry? Then you will need more glamorous color choices and combinations. A company or group that is tuned into the latest trends (such as show biz, cosmetics, hair styling, or retail clothing manufacturers) expect you to know what all of the "happening" colors are, and you will lose credibility if you come in wearing a sober Charcoal Gray, unless charcoal is the "new black" that season!

For any job interview, wear the colors appropriate to that business. If you have trouble coming up with color combinations, go back to chapter 3 for Goof-Proof combinations and chapter 4 for Signature Color advice.

If you are a woman and are presenting numbers to a heavy-duty group of budget directors, you don't want to look like the frosting on a birthday cake. The resistance you might get in a fluffy pink or blazing yellow suit the color of dandelions will be diminished if you wear a darker power color, such as Cappuccino, instead. Save the bit of pink fluff for the sweater under your suit or convert the dandelion to a classy piece of gold jewelry. While I deplore the idea that your intelligence will be in question if you wear a color you love and feel good in, it takes the type of audience described previously some time to work through the first impression and listen to what you have to say.

The same concept of power colors is equally important to men. However, if your destination is a seminar in Hawaii, you'll look pretty silly in a serious dark business suit and a lei, no matter how powerful the color.

As a color consultant, everyone expects me to deliver a talk in something colorful. My preference is to put an outfit together that consists of my personal Signature Colors. This always presents an attractive, coordinated picture—remember, the eyes of the audience are trained on you for the length of the presentation. Anything too busy or too blatantly bright can be visually disconcerting and won't do much for the content of your talk. It might help to keep them awake, but they will be slightly cross-eyed and visually tired by the time you've finished.

The fashion industry, especially cosmetics, often separates colors into groupings. Although they might not be referred to these groupings in the Colortime Sunrise, Sunlight, Sunset system, they often use essentially three palettes that are called simply cool, warm, and neutral. But those are just general terms, as the cool classifications often contain some warm and/or neutral tones, the warm category often has some cool and/or neutral tones, and the mid or neutral group expands to include additional, generally muted shades. So it can be very similar to the Colortime categories that are a good guide for your color selection.

Think of the displays you see in the stores or in magazine ads: Sunrise ocean greens and blues, ultramarines, and blushing pinks. Sunset painted desert shades of earthy reds, burnt coppers, hot pink, and warm corals. And the Sunlight, or so-called neutral palette, might contain typical neutrals like taupe and gray, but it can also include some soft peach, wild rose, jade green, and heavenly blue.

You'll more often see gold in the Sunset cosmetic palette, silver in the Sunrise, and for the Sunlight, a glimmery finish over a taupe shade. But just as with jewelry (see chapter 4), there are some interesting Crossovers that defy some of the old rigid rules about gold being the exclusive property of the warm category and silver always remaining cool (think burnished pewter tones rather than shiny cool silver finishes). And your jewelry might very well contain a combination of gold and silver, so that you have your choice of what to "play up" in your cosmetics. Cosmetics allow you to play with layering of colors and combining gold and silver finishes. Sunlight people, in particular, should play with layering; it's a great way to get just the right mix.

NOW TAKE A DEEP
BREATH AND OPEN
YOUR CLOSET DOOR

Image consultants will tell you that there is nothing they prefer to do for a client more than to rearrange, weed out, sort out, and recycle their closet. It's instant gratification for them and their client. They can also get some instant insight into a client's personality and lifestyle through the colors he or she wears. If you're like most people, opening your closet door and finding it neat, efficient, and attractive makes you feel so "together." Somehow, when your closet is organized, you feel as though your whole life is organized. (If only that were true!)

Whether you get professional help or do it yourself, the very best time to get your closet together is when you're redecorating or repainting. Everything is a mess anyhow, so a little more mess can't possibly hurt. You have to have everything out of the closet anyway, unless you're one of those sneaky people who repaint a whole house but never touch the fifty-year-old wallpaper in the closet. I view my closets in much the same way that my mother viewed clean underwear. You never know when you might be involved in an accident and get carted off to a hospital—and you just never know when a nearsighted dinner guest on the way to the powder room is going to walk into your closet!

The key to a wonderfully arranged closet is color. When you're really ready to get into it, the following guidelines can give you a plan of action.

To get started...

1. Pull out anything you haven't worn in a year and put it on the bed.

2. Separate day clothes from evening clothes, and put them in different sections of the closet.

3. Keep all of the same kinds of clothing together: all blouses and/or shirts, all pants, all skirts, all suits, etc.

4. Arrange all of these groups by color.

5. Throw away all your shoeboxes (unless you have X-ray vision) and put your shoes in see-through plastic containers. Writing on the outside of cardboard boxes doesn't work—you usually can't remember what the "black loafers" look like! Keep your shoes at eye level or above, if possible, so you don't have to crawl around on all fours groping for them. If you have the space, you may opt to keep your shoes on slanted shelving made specifically for shoes.

6. Organize your handbags, sweaters, socks and/or stockings, and underwear, and put them in see-through plastic containers on shelves. This is especially appropriate for hosiery and socks—it really takes the frustration out of fishing through the blacks, browns, and navies when you keep them separated by color.

7. Try to store as much as possible outside of bureau drawers. You might discover things in bureau drawers that you haven't seen in ages. If you don't see it, you don't use it. Haven't you ever brought something home from the store only to discover eventually that you had something just like it—that you had simply forgotten about it?

8. Get a piece of Peg-Board™ and assorted metal hanging hooks from your local hardware or building supply store. If your closet is big enough, put it up on a wall or on the back of a door. If you don't have that kind of space, use a bedroom, bathroom, or dressing room wall. This is where you'll hang your costume jewelry and belts—all organized by color on the metal hooks placed in the Peg-Board™. This is also a good place to hang odd things that don't seem to go anywhere else.

9. Put a piece of thin foam rubber over some wire hangers and hang your scarves or ties from them, arranged by color. They won't slide off, and you won't have to press the wrinkles out of your scarves every time you wear them.

If you can afford a professionally installed closet system, it is well worth the investment. If not, home building supply and hardware stores all stock the coated wire or solid shelving for do-it-yourself projects. If you're not handy in the hammer and toggle bolt department, find someone who is or your efforts to be well organized can turn into chaos. Trust me on that one—I've been there!

The ideal closet has double-hung rods so that you can keep your blouses or shirts hanging above your pants and/or skirts. Since everything should be arranged by color, you can readily see what you have in each color family. It's so much easier to see what goes with what.

To get back to that pile of clothes on the bed that you never wear, check them out to see why you aren't wearing them. Chances are you have nothing to wear them with—they're usually "bargains" that are not in your Colortime.

If you're not wearing them because they're just a little out of date, (wide lapels, narrow lapels), but they're classic, decide if alterations are really worth it, move them to another closet, or retire them permanently. If you have ever helped a "clothesaholic" friend and found him or her sneaking things back into the closet from that pile, the friend often wails, "But I wore that on my first date!" (fifteen years before).

When doing your own closet, you don't have to be brutal about getting rid of things. You can keep anything that has real sentimental value. But the whole point is to get organized and to give yourself more space, and there is always a local thrift shop or "dress for success" program that can benefit from your donation.

As you continue to buy clothing in your preferred Colortime palette, you'll see how much easier and more practical it is to combine, mix and match, and enjoy your clothes as well as your colors.

IF YOU CAN AFFORD A PROFESSIONALLY INSTALLED CLOSET SYSTEM, IT'S WELL WORTH THE INVESTMENT.

COLORS FOR THAT SPECIAL DAY

Has there ever been a bride who doesn't want her wedding day to be perfect? Of course, that includes looking radiant in the perfect dress. Choosing colors within your own Colortime can make your skin literally glow as you glide down the aisle on that special day.

Unless you are opting for a more unconventional color choice, chances are your dress will be some variation of white, off-white, cream, or ivory. But even in that narrow range, there are tints that flatter your coloring more than any others. You'll look beautiful on your wedding day as well as in the photos that record this really meaningful time in your life.

Here are some guidelines for choosing the best undertones:

Sunrise

As your skin tone is either very fair or really dark, or perhaps somewhat exotic as in Asian, Latina, or Indian, the cooler whites either enhance or contrast with your coloring. Yours are the clearest, most dazzling, purest whites you can find. And if you have blue or very dark eyes, a bluish undertone to that snow white makes the white seem even cooler.

Sunlight

Not too cool and not too warm, ivory whites and off-whites (with a smidgen of rose, green, or blue) offer you a really big choice. Your skin type has many alternatives, especially since your complexion is a beautiful blend of warmth and coolness. If you're brown-eyed, it's best to lean toward warm undertones; if your eyes are blue, try something a bit cooler. And chameleon green eyes change according to the colors that are reflected in them.

Sunset

Warm undertones set your skin aglow. Your best whites should always veer toward the warm side. Creamy whites blend beautifully with your creamy or mocha-type complexions. And if you're a golden blonde, honey brown, or redhead, the peachy whites work wonders. Even if you have blue eyes, they're not as cool as Sunrise and might even have little warm flecks in them.

Your personal Colortime can also set the stage for the ceremony and reception. Use your Colortime combinations to create the table settings and floral displays and to dress the other members of the wedding party. Since the wedding party needs to dress harmoniously, this is not the time for individual color choices. The most important decision is: what Colortime will be the dominant theme? The colors create the ambiance (and, again, the beautiful photographs) that everyone remembers.

The bride traditionally gets to choose the colors. Ideally, she confers with everyone involved, but she has the final word. Invariably, the bride chooses her own favorite Colortime. I've rarely seen it work any other way, unless there is a very domineering Mama or Mama-in-law involved.

Many grooms are now demanding equal say and playing a part in the whole process. Eventually (usually) everybody agrees and they all live happily ever after. However, it doesn't always happen that way. One couple asked me to arbitrate because they couldn't decide on wedding colors, furniture for the apartment, or the color of the car they were going to share.

He was a Sunset and she was a Sunrise and both were very definite about their likes and dislikes. They compromised on the Sunlight palette, which seemed to satisfy them both. They invited me to the wedding. A few weeks later, however, I was uninvited. It seems that colors were not the only thing they couldn't agree on.

Most everyone in the wedding party can find a color in the Sunlight palette that pleases him or her and whose subtlety suits the occasion. Crossover Colors are also a good compromise. Bridesmaids in deep wine velvets and ushers in gray have become traditional in winter weddings.

Coordinate your flowers and table linens with the wedding party colors, and everything will be beautiful. When you look back at the wedding pictures in years to come, it will have been worth all the effort.

I am reminded of one Hollywood wedding—the bride and the groom shall remain nameless—where the bride wore a lace dress that must have been inspired by *Gone With the Wind*. It was miles of blush--colored lace over an enormous hoop skirt. She also wore a huge picture hat.

There was barely enough room for her father to walk down the aisle with her, so he sort of trailed behind. It took the groom what seemed like a full five minutes to maneuver around the skirt with its big hoop, so that he barely reached her lips for the final kiss and almost knocked her hat off.

Her attendants all wore whatever colors they chose—a variety of vivid shades. It was definitely not what you would call subtle.

For confirmation parties, Sweet Sixteens, Bar and Bat mitzvahs, and other special events, the Colortime used should be the one favored by the honoree. The Colortime theme can start with the invitations and carry through the flowers and the rest of the decor.

If you're planning the party, and the Colortime used isn't your favorite, keep an open mind. Fashion coordinators and interior designers learn how to please their clients and often use colors they don't find pleasing personally.

After the Colortime is chosen, you decide on the dominant and subordinate colors within that Colortime. Then you refer to the color wheel to decide how you want to combine your colors. The procedure is much the same as that used in decorating a home.

You must decide whether you are going to use:

- One dominant color (monochromatic)
- Two colors (one dominant and the other subordinate)
- Three colors (one dominant, the second subordinate, the third, a touch)
- Multicolor (polychromatic)—a mixture of colors within a print or pattern. Select one color from within the mix and use it as the major accent color

Remember that analogous colors are easy to combine. The complementaries are the most attention-getting and fun when used in the brightest intensities.

Don't let the terminology scare you. Go back to chapter 3 and look at the Goof-Proof combinations. Use a color board to show all the colors. It really does help to use color swatches to represent linens, flowers, candles, etc., just to see how the combination will look. It really is a fun, creative, exercise. It's just like being back in kindergarten with your paste and baby scissors (the kind you could never cut with). It's also marvelous therapy after a long, harrowing day. You may like it so much that you continue to do paste-ups and get seriously into scrap-booking after your party is over and you're left with wonderful memories, a photo album, and, of course, the bills.

9

YOUR CREATIVE ENERGIES AND COLOR

In this chapter, you'll find out more about your color preferences. It's only natural for you to like some individual colors in your Colortime palette much more than others. Luckily, if you really dislike a color, it probably won't be in your Colortime. Though every color family appears in each Colortime, the intensities and values vary, and you're bound to have different emotional responses.

That's why I always listen carefully to each client and try to determine his or her orientation to different colors before making recommendations. Unfortunately, I can't be with you personally, but I can share certain universal concepts to make some useful observations about your personal color choices.

Please remember that your likes and dislikes can change during different periods of your life. Your responses simply tell you where you are in your life right now. Your preferences may also indicate some of your secret desires. For example, red is considered the most ardent and passionate of all colors. You may not see yourself as ardent or passionate, but if red is your favorite color, maybe you have hidden traits just dying to be expressed (you little devil!).

Red

LIKE:

Just as red sits on top of the rainbow, you like to stay on top of things. You have a zest for life. Remember that red can speed up the pulse, increase the respiration rate, and raise blood pressure. It is associated with fire, heat, and blood, so it is impossible to ignore. And so are you (or would like to be). You are high maintenance and high profile, a mover and a shaker.

The key words associated with red are winner, achiever, intense, impulsive, active, competitive, daring, aggressive. Red people are exciting, animated, optimistic, emotional, and extroverted. Desire is the key word (see "ardent" and "passionate" above), so you hunger for fullness of experience and living. Red is a force to be reckoned with and is always up for adventure. Your passion is infectious.

You are an exciting person to be with, and always stimulating. The world would be a dull place without red people.

Now that you have all the good news, let's hear it for the bad news. Since you crave so much excitement in your life, routine can drive you nuts. Restlessness can make you fickle in your pursuit of new things to turn you on. It's hard for you to be objective, and you can be opinionated and overbearing. You have a tendency to listen to what others tell you and then do whatever you please. Patience is not one of your virtues. If you're unhappy about something—watch out!

DISLIKE:

Since red is primarily associated with a zest for life, excitement, and passion, disliking this hue could mean that these feelings are a bit much for you to handle at this point in your life. Perhaps you are bothered by the aggressiveness and intensity that red signifies. Or perhaps you really want more fulfillment but are afraid to get involved. People who are irritable, ill, exhausted, or bothered by many problems often reject red and turn to the calmer colors for rest and relaxation. They are very self-protective.

Pink

LIKE:

This is a softened red, so it tempers passion with purity. There is no blatant sensuality in pink as there can be in red. Pink is associated with romance, sweetness, delicacy, refinement, and tenderness. Pink people are interested in the world around them, but they don't throw themselves into participating with the ardor of the red person. While red is assertive, pink is gentle. Violence in any form is upsetting to you.

At one time, pink was considered quintessentially feminine, like the frosting on a little girl's birthday cake, but now it can be worn by men without embarrassment—after all, it is closely related to red.

If you love pink, you are talented though not overly ambitious. You are charming and warm and are probably an incurable romantic who enjoys creating ceremonies and special occasions. Pink people are friendly but tend to keep their inner feelings hidden, as they often sublimate that bit of red that sometimes peeks through.

DISLIKE:

Some people are simply indifferent to pink. It is sweetness, innocence, and naiveté—red with the passion removed. So if you dislike pink, you're looking for excitement in your life, and pink simply doesn't do it for you.

The closer to orange pink gets, the warmer it is, and the warmer you are.

Yellow

LIKE:

Yellow is luminous and warm because it is strongly associated with sunshine. It sparkles with outgoing activity. Yellow people are highly original, innovative, imaginative, idealistic, creative, artistic, and often spiritual. You love novelty and challenge and have an inquiring mind. You are a reliable friend and confidant. You are optimistic and encourage others to do their best, so your friends love your "up" attitude. Your ambitions are often realized, and you usually have a sunny disposition, which makes you a fun "playmate."

You are often egotistical, however, and don't like to be second best. You can be generous, but you may be rather shy and appear somewhat aloof as a result. You may be impatient with other people's ideas if they seem less well thought out than yours. You are genuinely concerned about the good of society, but you generally spend more time talking about it than actually doing anything about it! Yellow people are perfectionists, but they can also be joyful.

DISLIKE:

If you dislike yellow, you usually dislike the qualities of this luminous color. You are a realist—a practical, down-to-earth person and probably critical of others who are not. You are skeptical of new ideas, and rather than try something innovative, you prefer to concentrate on things you know you can accomplish. Guaranteed results are important to you, because you like to protect yourself from disappointment.

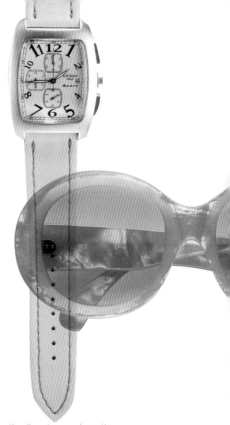

If yellow is your favorite, you never say: "Been there, done that."

Orange

LIKE:

Orange is a combination of red and yellow, so it takes on many of the characteristics of both colors. It is vibrant and warm, like a glorious sunset. Orange has the physical force of red, but it is less intense, passionate, and assertive. Lovers of this color work and play hard, are adventurous and enthusiastic, are always looking for new worlds to conquer.

You are good-natured, expansive, and extroverted, with a disposition as bright as your favorite color, and you like to be with people. Your ideas are unique and you are very determined. You are more agreeable than aggressive, and people are drawn to you because of your warmth, energy, and magnetism. Gregarious could be your middle name.

But orange people can be fickle. It has been said that your latest friend is your best friend. Some experts contend that men whose favorite color is orange are the worst possible kind to marry. They are said to be great fun and good mixers but undependable, flaky types. Of course, the same could be said of women. Maybe you'd better check out someone's favorite color before you get involved!

Success in business can come easily to this outgoing, charming person, who has a great sense of humor. Since orange is a physical and mental stimulant, start the day by eating an orange while dressed in your orange terry bathrobe, to start your mind and body working together!

DISLIKE:

Life is definitely not a dish of gumdrops for the person who rejects orange. Nothing flamboyant appeals to you. You dislike too much partying, hilarity, loud laughter, showing off, and obvious intimacy. As a result, you may be difficult to get to know, if not a loner. You prefer a few genuine close friends to a large circle of acquaintances, and once you make a friend, that person is your friend forever.

Brown

LIKE:

The color of Mother Earth is the hue associated with substance, stability, and real sense of worth. A preference for brown means you have a steady, reliable character with a keen sense of duty and responsibility. You are the down-to-earth person with a subtle sense of humor. Browns love simplicity, comfort, quality, harmony, hearth, and home.

You are a loyal friend—understanding but firm. Brown people have strong views and may be intolerant of others who think, talk, or act too quickly. You strive to be good money managers (we won't say "cheap"), drive a good bargain, and demand the best quality you can get. Quality is a key word, so it's not all about organic and homespun; there is a striving for the best that money can buy.

You might find it difficult to be carefree and spontaneous, but you often rebel internally against accepting things the way they are. You feel very uncomfortable about losing control, but will work hard to change a situation that seems unjust or unfair.

You'll make a good marriage partner and a good parent because you have a strong need for security and a sense of belonging. Family life is very important to you.

DISLIKE:

You probably fantasize about a lot of things, perhaps traveling with a circus or racing cars. Novelty excites you, and routine drives you crazy. You are witty, impetuous, and generous. Living on a farm is not for you, and homespun people bore you. You do like people, but they must be bright and outgoing. A meaningful relationship with you might be risky business—it's hard to get you to sit still!

Beige

LIKE:

Beige people have many of the same characteristics as brown people do, though they are probably less intense. Creamy beiges and honeyed tones take on a lot of yellow qualities, while rose beiges take on pink characteristics. You are warm, appreciate quality, and are carefully neutral in most situations. You are usually well adjusted and practical, preferring traditional or classic looks to trendiness.

DISLIKE:

You are less frenetic and impetuous than one who dislikes brown, but you have many of the same characteristics. To you, beige represents a beige existence—boring and tiresome. You hate routine.

Green

LICK:

LIKE:

Nature's most plentiful color promises a balance between warmth and coolness, so green people are usually stable, balanced types. You are the good citizen, concerned parent, involved neighbor, and PTA member—the joiner of clubs and organizations. You are fastidious, kind, and generous, especially with your time, and you're a good listener.

It's important for you to win the admiration of peers, so you are often a "do-gooder." You are a caring companion, a loyal friend, partner, or lover, with a high moral sense and are supersensitive about doing the right thing. Occasionally you can be a little preachy.

You are intelligent and understand new concepts. You are less inclined, however, to risk something new than to do what is popular and conventional. The worst vice for a green is the tendency to gossip. Are you a little green with envy?

DISLIKE:

Since lovers of green are usually very social types, those who dislike green often put those qualities down. You may have an unfulfilled need to be recognized that causes you to pull away from people rather than joining them. You don't like thinking, looking, and doing things the way you see the majority of people thinking, looking, and doing them. Company picnics, cocktail parties, conventions in Las Vegas, and office parties are not your thing as you are a bit "detached."

Biliousness and certain bodily functions are often associated with yellow-green, as are snakes, lizards, dragons, and various other creepy-crawlies. Did something slithery frighten you as a child?

Blue

LIKE:

The color of tranquility and peace, blue tends to be the most preferred color. Although cool and confident (or wishing to be), blues can be vulnerable. You are trusting and need to be trusted. You are sensitive to the needs of others and form strong attachments and are deeply hurt if your trust has been betrayed.

Blue people aspire to harmony, serenity, patience, perseverance, and peace and have a calming influence on other people. You are somewhat social but prefer sticking to your own close circle of friends. You think twice before speaking or acting. You are generally conservative, even-tempered, and reliable, a team player and good co-worker. People are drawn to you because you are so discreet and loyal—great traits in a friend.

Because of the highly developed sense of responsibility of the blue personality, you must be careful of perfectionist tendencies that may make you unrealistically demanding. Your gentleness, however, wins out.

If you have trouble falling asleep at night, count blue sheep.

DISLIKE:

A dislike of blue may mean restlessness—a need to break away from the sameness that bores you. Perhaps you want to change your job, or even your life, and long for more excitement. You may be tired of being "depended on," but your conscience makes you stay. You wish that you were wealthy or brilliant (or both), because that would enable you to have all the good things in life without working so hard. Deeper blues may mean sadness and melancholy to you—blue may simply give you the blues.

Blue-Green

LIKE:

Since this is a marriage of the colors mentioned above, many of the traits are combined, but there are added dimensions. You are neat (to the point of fussiness) and well groomed. You are sensitive, but also sophisticated, self-assured, and (usually) stable.

You help others and usually manage your own affairs very well. Courtesy and charm are characteristic of you, too. But narcissism is a key word here. Green-blues love to dress up to elicit the admiration of others; but along with admiration, you may provoke some of the "blue-green-eyed monsters."

DISLIKE:

Since love of blue-green means orderliness and neatness, dislike of blue-green means that, as messy as you'd like to be, a little voice inside you (was it your mother or your father?) keeps telling you to clean up your room. As much as you try to ignore that little voice, it doesn't go away. You really love to relax more and not pay attention to petty details, and you prefer earthy types to fussy people.

Purple

LIKE:

This hue has an aura of mystery and intrigue. The purple person is enigmatic and highly creative, with a quick perception of spiritual ideas. Purple is often preferred by artists or people who support the arts. Those who like to consider themselves unconventional or different from the common herd often prefer purple. Mystical things or concepts hold great appeal for these dreamers. The red part of purple often turns the dreams and ideas into reality. Lovers of purple see new solutions through new perspectives.

You are often generous and, at times, charming. Purple is also associated with wit, keen observation, super sensitivity, vanity, and moodiness. Because purple is a combination of red and blue, which are opposites in many ways, you often have conflicting traits. You constantly try to balance those opposites—the excitement of red with the tranquility of blue. It has been said that purple people are easy to live with but hard to know. You can be secretive, so that even when you seem to confide freely, your closest friends may say they don't always understand you.

DISLIKE:

If you are antipurple, you need sincerity, honesty, and a lack of pretense in your life. You don't like to get involved unless you know exactly what you're getting yourself into. You usually exercise good judgment, and frankness is a quality you look for in your friends. You may not have any particular artistic talent, but you make a good critic!

Because of purple's association with royalty, this color may seem puffed up and pompous to you, or because of its association with mourning, you may see it as melancholy. In certain parts of the world, bright purple is worn by ladies of questionable reputation. Perhaps you're still hearing that little voice in your ear telling you that nice people don't wear purple.

Lavender

LIKE:

People who love this tint sometimes use it to the exclusion of all other colors. Just as with the purple lover, this person likes to be considered different. You are quick-witted though usually not overly intellectual.

The lavender person seeks refinement in life and is often a bit naive. Yours is a fantasy land where ugliness and the baser aspects of life are ignored or denied. Outward appearances are very important. Gentility and sentimental leanings also go along with this color, as do romance, nostalgia, and delicacy.

DISLIKE:

Yours is a no-nonsense approach to life. You don't like others to be coy with you—you prefer them to be direct. Nostalgia is not your thing; you live in the present. Just as with the anti-purple people, you don't like superficiality in manners or appearance, and you usually let people know about it (or wish that you had). You may also see lavender as insipid or aging.

Since lavender is a first cousin of purple, you may aspire to creativity, but even if you're not capable of it, you tend to encourage those who do have talent.

Gray

LIKE:

People who prefer this most neutral of all shades are carefully neutral about life. You like to protect yourself from the hectic world, wrapping yourself in the security blanket of a noncommittal color. You prefer a secure, safe, balanced existence, and so, unlike the reds in life, you never crave real excitement, just contentment. It is important for you to maintain the status quo.

You often make compromises in your lifestyle. You are practical and calm and do not like to attract attention. You are willing to work hard (the gray flannel suit) and to be of service. You are the middle-of-the-road type—cool, conservative, composed, and reliable. You are the solid rock on whom others rely. If this makes you feel a little boring, the consolation is that you often use a splash of color to make some sort of statement. So you really aren't all that dull!

DISLIKE:

To dislike gray is to dislike neutrality. You would rather be right or wrong, but never indifferent. Routine bores you; you look for a richer, fuller life. This may lead you to one involvement, hobby, or interest after another in the pursuit of happiness. Gray may mean eerie ghosts, ashes, cobwebs, and the dust of a haunted house or other scary gray things.

Taupe

LIKE:

This color also speaks of neutrality, but it combines the character and dependability of gray with the warmth of beige. You like classic looks and are careful about allowing too much excitement into your life. You are practical, fair, and well balanced, and you make a good arbitrator.

DISLIKE:

If taupe doesn't appeal to you, it may be because it is *so* balanced and classic. You prefer to make a more definite statement, whether with color or something else. You're probably not known for your subtlety.

White

LIKE:

White is cleanliness, purity, and complete simplicity. Those who prefer white are neat and immaculate in their clothing and homes, with everything in its place and well organized. You are inclined to be a cautious buyer and shrewd trader, but you are critical and fussy. If you got a spot on your tie or your scarf in a restaurant, you ask for a glass of water immediately to clean it off, so white signifies a self-sufficient person. But white can also mean a longing to be young again, to return to a time of innocence and new beginnings.

DISLIKE:

Since white represents cleanliness and purity, to dislike white does not exactly mean that you are a messy person, but it does mean that you have never been obsessed with order. You are not very fussy. Things that are a little off-center are much more interesting to you than those that are perfectly in line. A little dust on the shelves or on yourself doesn't propel you into a spasm of cleaning. You are not very uptight and are easy to be with. White to you is too sterile and cold.

Black

LIKE:

This is rarely chosen as a favorite color because it is actually the negation of color. The person who chooses black may have a number of conflicting attitudes. You may be conventional, conservative, and serious, or you may like to think of yourself as rather worldly or sophisticated, a cut above everyone else, or very dignified.

You may also want to have an air of mystery, intensity, or, as in the language of the proverbial black negligee, be very sexy. Wit, cleverness, personal security, and prestige are very important to you. Black is the most powerful of colors, and you feel empowered when you wear it.

DISLIKE:

Since black is the negation of color, it may be a total negative to you. It is the eternal mystery, the bottomless pit, the black hole, the Halloween witch and her black cat. It may represent death and mourning to you. Things that go bump in the night are black. Were you frightened by the dark in your childhood? That experience could be buried in the darkest recesses of your mind and may still haunt you when you look at anything black.

Black may simply be too heavy or depressing for you to handle at this point in your life. You are uncomfortable with the super sophisticated and feel insecure in their company. You like real people and are not dazzled by fame.

If your favorite (or least favorite) is actually a combination color—such as Caramel, which is a combination of brown and orange—you have some of the traits of both hues and a more complex personality. Some of these characteristics may actually seem in conflict with each other. For example, brown is focused on family life, whereas orange can be fickle. How much of you is orange and how much is brown?

The closer to its neighbor a color gets, the more it takes on the personality of that color. A red-purple is more exciting than a blue-purple; a yellow-orange is happier than a yellow-green.

Lightening a hue takes some of the strength out of it. For example, if one of your favorites is a cream color, this is the lightest combination of yellow and brown. It never sparkles the way yellow does because it has been paled, yet the effect can still be cheering and warm. The more yellow you add, the happier the color is and so are you.

Darkening a hue adds dignity, depth, and strength. Shades like wine, dark greens, deep purple, navy blue, and charcoal gray take the basic characteristics of those hues and make them more conservative, refined, and restrained. For example, deep wine reds like Beaujolais are positive and assured, but certainly more dignified than fiery Fiesta Red.

Watch TV commercials to see how color is used on spokespeople. A man in a dark jacket and subtle tie convinces you to buy various kinds of aspirin or to put your money in his hands. His clothes give him more credibility than he would have in a neon-bright sweater.

Many people who have remade their lives choose new colors to go with their new selves: people who are in periods of change, often after a breakup with a significant other or a career change. They feel like throwing everything away and starting all over again. I wouldn't suggest anything that drastic. Besides, it's too expensive. But if you're reinventing your life, maybe this is also the best time to reinvent your colors.

REINVENT YOUR LIFE
REINVENT YOUR COLORS.

more alive with color

CONCLUSION

Unless you live in a cave or a nudist camp, you have to wear clothes. Every day of your life you send messages out via your personal colors. Why not choose your very best colors for those messages, whether you're wearing a work outfit, party clothes, or around-the-house weekend fun stuff? You're painting a picture for your own enjoyment that can't help but spill over onto those around you.

Use your colortime palette as an expression of you, to help you feel more rested, energized, creative, and confident, and to make your clothing a true source of comfort. You deserve it.

I hope this book has given you useful and enjoyable information. Your life may never be the same. You may find yourself studying the celebrities on TV or the person in front of you at the checkout stand and driving your friends, family, and salespeople crazy with your newfound knowledge. (Careful—lighting and makeup can be deceptive, so what you're seeing on the TV screen or in the movies may be reel coloring instead of real coloring!) You're apt to look at the colors they choose—for their clothes, makeup, and hair—with a new perspective. It can be great fun and a wonderful way to heighten your awareness of the world around you.

Use your Colortime palette as an expression of the real you, chosen from the Colortime that makes you look and feel your absolute best. Make every day a special day ... come more alive—with color!

pantone color index

Fashion and home professionals worldwide recognize the PANTONE Textile Color System® as the global communication tool for color specification. Today, hundreds of thousands of designers, product managers, merchandisers and quality control professionals rely on Pantone, Inc. to ensure that their color selections for product development are communicated accurately. Use the perforated Colortime Concepts™ palettes to take with you when traveling, shopping, or just out and about.

Almond Blossom	PANTONE 13-2006	Cendre Blue	PANTONE 17-4131
Amber Yellow	PANTONE 13-0942	Ceramic	PANTONE 16-5127
Amethyst Orchid	PANTONE 17-3628	Cerise	PANTONE 19-1955
Apricot Cream	PANTONE 13-1027	Charcoal Gray	PANTONE 18-0601
Baroque Rose	PANTONE 18-1634	Chardonnay	PANTONE 13-0633
Beach Glass	PANTONE 13-5412	Chateau Gray	PANTONE 15-4503
Beaujolais	PANTONE 18-2027	Cloud Gray	PANTONE 15-3802
Bellini	PANTONE 13-1114	Cognac	PANTONE 18-1421
Beryl Green	PANTONE 16-5515	Confetti	PANTONE 16-1723
Bisque	PANTONE 13-1109	Coriander	PANTONE 17-1113
Bleached Sand	PANTONE 13-1008	Cornflower Blue	PANTONE 16-4031
Blue Atoll	PANTONE 16-4535	Cornsilk	PANTONE 13-0932
Blue Bell	PANTONE 14-4121	Cranberry	PANTONE 17-1545
Blue Iris	PANTONE 18-3943	Custard	PANTONE 13-0720
Blue Jewel	PANTONE 18-4535	Cyclamen	PANTONE 16-3118
Blue Turquoise	PANTONE 15-5217	Daiquiri Green	PANTONE 12-0435
Blush	PANTONE 15-1614	Dark Earth	PANTONE 19-1020
Blushing Bride	PANTONE 12-1310	Deep Mahogany	PANTONE 19-1420
Bonnie Blue	PANTONE 16-4134	Deep Peacock Blue	PANTONE 17-5029
Bougainvillea	PANTONE 17-3725	Deep Periwinkle	PANTONE 17-3932
Bright Chartreuse	PANTONE 14-0445	Deep Taupe	PANTONE 18-1312
Bright Rose	PANTONE 18-1945	Deep Ultramarine	PANTONE 19-3950
Bright White	PANTONE 11-0601	Delft	PANTONE 19-4039
Burlwood	PANTONE 17-1516	Della Robbia Blue	PANTONE 16-4020
Burnt Coral	PANTONE 16-1529	Desert Rose	PANTONE 17-1927
Butterfly	PANTONE 12-0322	Doe	PANTONE 16-1333
Byzantium	PANTONE 19-3138	Dusty Lavender	PANTONE 17-3313
Cadmium Orange	PANTONE 15-1340	Earth Red	PANTONE 18-1631
Camel	PANTONE 17-1224	Eggplant	PANTONE 19-2311
Cameo Green	PANTONE 14-6312	Electric Green	PANTONE 14-5721
Cameo Pink	PANTONE 14-2307	Emerald	PANTONE 17-5641
Cappuccino	PANTONE 19-1220	Faded Denim	PANTONE 17-4021
Capri Breeze	PANTONE 17-4735	Fair Green	PANTONE 15-6316
Caramel	PANTONE 16-1439	Feldspar	PANTONE 16-5815
Cayenne	PANTONE 18-1651	Fern	PANTONE 16-0430
Celestial	PANTONE 18-4530	Fiesta	PANTONE 17-1564

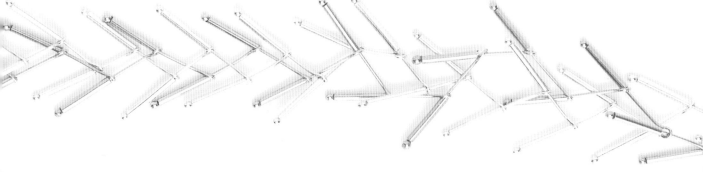

Fir	PANTONE 18-5621	Persian Jewel	PANTONE 17-3934
Frost Gray	PANTONE 17-0000	Pesto	PANTONE 18-0228
Ginger	PANTONE 17-1444	Petit Four	PANTONE 14-4516
Glacier Gray	PANTONE 14-4102	Pineneedle	PANTONE 19-5920
Gossamer Pink	PANTONE 13-1513	Pink Icing	PANTONE 15-1717
Grape Nectar	PANTONE 18-1710	Placid Blue	PANTONE 15-3920
Grape Royale	PANTONE 19-3518	Powder Pink	PANTONE 14-1511
Gray Dawn	PANTONE 14-4106	Prism Pink	PANTONE 14-2311
Green Haze	PANTONE 14-0615	Prism Violet	PANTONE 19-3748
Green Moss	PANTONE 17-0636	Purple Haze	PANTONE 18-3718
Honey Gold	PANTONE 15-1142	Raspberry Radiance	PANTONE 19-2432
Hot Chocolate	PANTONE 19-1325	Red Violet	PANTONE 17-1818
Ibis Rose	PANTONE 17-2520	Rose Dust	PANTONE 14-1307
Infinity	PANTONE 17-4015	Sachet Pink	PANTONE 15-2216
Iris Orchid	PANTONE 17-3323	Sauterne	PANTONE 15-0942
Jadeite	PANTONE 16-5304	Sea Pink	PANTONE 15-1912
Jet Black	PANTONE 19-0303	Seagrass	PANTONE 16-6008
Jojoba	PANTONE 14-0935	Sepia	PANTONE 18-0928
Lattè	PANTONE 15-1220	Shocking Pink	PANTONE 17-2127
Lavender	PANTONE 15-3817	Silver Lake Blue	PANTONE 17-4030
Light Taupe	PANTONE 16-1210	Simply Taupe	PANTONE 16-0906
Lilac Marble	PANTONE 14-3903	Sky Blue	PANTONE 14-4318
Lilac Snow	PANTONE 13-3405	Snorkel Blue	PANTONE 19-4049
Linden Green	PANTONE 15-0533	Sparkling Grape	PANTONE 19-3336
Little Boy Blue	PANTONE 16-4132	Sphinx	PANTONE 16-1703
Living Coral	PANTONE 16-1546	Spring Bouquet	PANTONE 14-6340
Magenta Haze	PANTONE 18-2525	Sunburst	PANTONE 13-1030
Mauve Mist	PANTONE 15-3207	Sunkist Coral	PANTONE 17-1736
Mellow Buff	PANTONE 13-1014	Sunlight	PANTONE 13-0822
Mimosa	PANTONE 14-0848	Taupe Gray	PANTONE 17-0808
Mirage Gray	PANTONE 15-4703	Teal	PANTONE 17-4919
Moonlight Blue	PANTONE 18-4027	Terra Cotta	PANTONE 16-1526
Moonlite Mauve	PANTONE 16-2614	Tigerlily	PANTONE 17-1456
Moonstruck	PANTONE 14-4500	True Red	PANTONE 19-1664
Moroccan Blue	PANTONE 19-4241	Verdant Green	PANTONE 19-6026
Muted Clay	PANTONE 16-1330	Very Berry	PANTONE 18-2336
Navy Blue	PANTONE 19-3832	Violet Tulle	PANTONE 16-3416
Neutral Gray	PANTONE 17-4402	Vista Blue	PANTONE 15-3930
Nile Blue	PANTONE 15-5210	Vivid Viola	PANTONE 18-3339
Nirvana	PANTONE 17-3808	Viola	PANTONE 16-3815
Palace Blue	PANTONE 18-4043	Warm Taupe	PANTONE 16-1318
Pale Khaki	PANTONE 15-1216	Weeping Willow	PANTONE 15-0525
Pampas	PANTONE 14-0826	Whisper White	PANTONE 11-0701
Peach	PANTONE 14-1227	Wild Rose	PANTONE 16-1715
Peach Parfait	PANTONE 14-1219	Winter Pear	PANTONE 15-0523
Peaches N' Cream	PANTONE 14-1521	Winter Wheat	PANTONE 14-1119
Pearled Ivory	PANTONE 11-0907	Winter White	PANTONE 11-0507
Peony	PANTONE 15-1816	Woodrose	PANTONE 16-1806

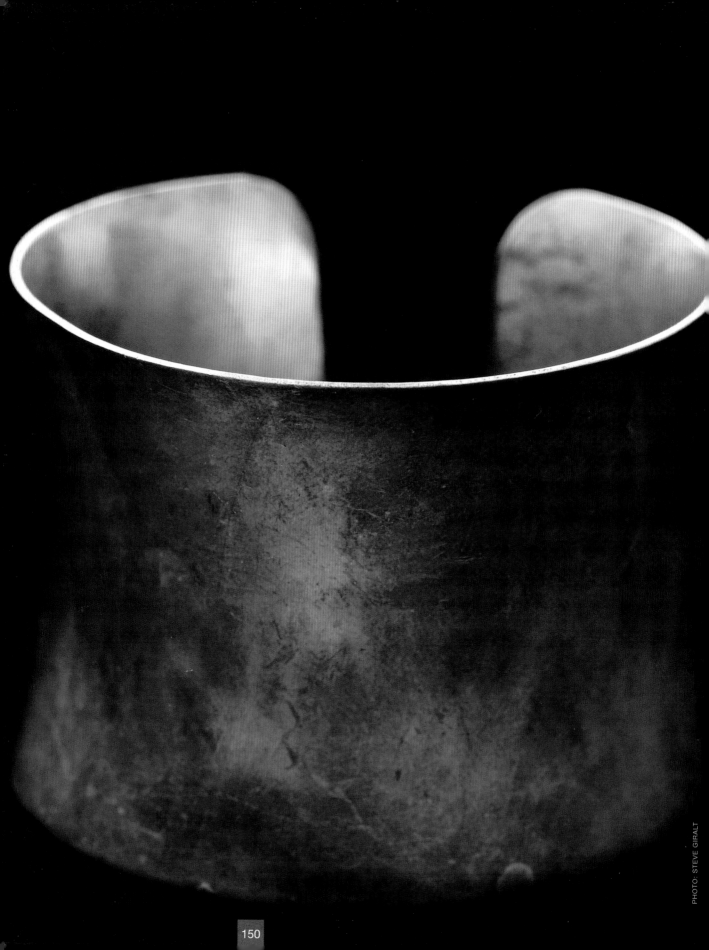

special thanks to the following

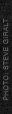
PHOTO: STEVE GIRALT

Art Direction & Design
Sean Zindren and
Kristian Bjornard
www.zindrendesign.com

Cover Design
Platinum Design
www.platinumdesign.com

Wardrobe & Styling
Jessica Zindren
www.jessicazindren.com

Hair & Make-up Styling
Sara Montiel
for Face Stockholm
missmontiel@earthlink.net
assisted by:
Pei-Shan Yuhasz

Original Photography
Gregory Boyd
www.gregboyd.com
Steven Girault
www.stevengirualt.com
Don Paulson
www.donpaulson.com

Thanks To The Following Designers and Retailers:
18 Karat; Paul Fredrick's Menswear; Donna Line Jewelry;
Laurie Kanyar Jewelry; Twin Cities Closets; Face Stockholm;
Teresa Goodall

Interested in more information about Colortime Concepts™?
- Books
- Products
- Professional Training
Visit www.colorexpert.com; or
Contact: leatrice@nwlink.com
We look forward to hearing from you…

index

index continued